5 - 9 - 09

To Pat (Cooper's Mom)

Much Love,
Christopher L. Brown

Pawriffic Training

Christopher L. Brown

Table of Contents

Acknowledgement

This is my first book. It is extremely important to me that pet owners read and understand this book. This book will promote a better relationship between dogs and their owners. It is a good book for first time dog owners as well for seasoned dog owners. This book will be a life saver for those all around the world who need help in the training of their pet.

I could not have done all of this alone. So I would like to take some time out to thank those that helped me with this book. First, I would like to thank God for giving me the ability to get this book done, and for giving me the love of animals, especially dogs, so that I am able to train them well. Without God's help, this book would not exist.

I want to give credit to the late Pet Trainer Susan Zeretzky. She was the first professional pet trainer to take me under her wings and mentor me. Susan was a great trainer. She knew how to handle all types of dogs. I wish she could see how far I have come. She gave me tough love. Everybody needs that somewhere in their career. I only got to know her for about seven months. In that short time, she taught me much of what I know today. Before she died, she told me to work under at least five trainers; take their ideas, and then become the best pet trainer that I could be. I cannot say it enough. "Thank you, Susan".

Another great person I want to give credit to is Patricia Jones. She was a high school teacher of mine that has known me my whole life. I keep in touch with her to this day. She helped with the initial review of my book. Sis Jones, you have helped many young adults move forward in life. Even though Patricia Jones never had a student who became a pet trainer, she believed in me and took a lot of her time out to help me with my book.

Much praise and respect to Dr. Furman, Dr. Factor, and their teams at their veterinarian offices. These vets do not work together, but they have both been firm believers in my style of training dogs for many years now. All of their patients say nothing but great things about them. Thank you guys!

Next are the clients. You guys are the best! I'm sure you know this, but I love you all. I have made special connections with all of my clients and their dogs. Every time I need you guys you are always there for me. Thank you for all the pictures, gifts, and tips, and thank you for helping me come up with a name for my book. As I was writing this book, many of you told me that if I ever needed anything at all to help my book or my career to just let you know, and consider it done. You all are the best. As long as I'm alive I will always be here for you guys. If I started naming those that have helped me, that would be unfair. I'm sure I would forget a name. You know who you are. Thank you!

Thank you, Tim Thimsen, for all that you have done for me. Tim Thimsen, CBC, CPDT is a full time trainer and behavior counselor. It was a treat training dogs with Tim. He has a great knowledge of dogs and their behavior. Tim has also helped me with my book. He was a big help in teaching me the business side of training dogs.

I have to give credit to my family and friends for all that they have done. I'm the first dog specialist of the Brown family. They supported me my whole journey while working with dogs. They do not get annoyed when I talk about dogs all day. My friends and family did not laugh at me in first grade when I told them I wanted to train dogs for a living. If they did, I might not have become a pet trainer.

There is one more person that I must thank. And that is you. I appreciate that you took time out of your day to read my first book. I don't know what part of the world you live in, but if you followed all in the instructions of the book and profited from it, then it has been a pleasure having you as a client too. Thank you!

Preface

Sometimes you see a dog you just love, but situations in your life do not allow you have a dog at this time. You, being human, look into those big brown eyes and get drawn in; and, therefore, you adopt a new member into your family. This new member you have just adopted into the family- you love him to death, but he just does not obey like you want him to. You have a great love for your dog, but you are beginning to notice something. And that is, you do not really know what you need to know about dogs to raise the one you have the right way.

What is your case?

- Did you use to have a dog as a child, loved him, but forgot how he was trained?

- Did you have a dog that you cared for from a puppy until his last days; and now have a new puppy; and this dog is totally different, and you do not know what to do?

- Is this your very first time having a dog or puppy and you're just clueless on what to do?

- Maybe all the dogs you have had were adopted as adults and you never had a puppy before.

- Do you know much about dogs but need a refresher on the basics?

- Or are you an upcoming dog trainer trying to get as much knowledge as possible?

If any of these cases fit your situation, you are going to enjoy reading this book. I understand your situation. You want to be able to train your new family member and learn more about him. You want to be able to know why he does some of the things that he does.

Sometimes getting into a pet training program or having somebody come to your home and train your dog can be a little stressful. Maybe the pet training program you want to get your dog into is too far away from your home, or they do not have any openings that fit your schedule, or the next class that does fit your schedule is a few weeks to maybe even a few months away. I feel that some pet training programs that come on television are fun to watch, but I noticed that most of them leave many facts out that every pet parent needs to know. It can also be hard to find a reputable trainer to come to your home. Well, within this reputable book, the training runs on your schedule.

ENJOY YOUR TRAINING!!

CHAPTER 1

(Week 1)

What is important right now is to know what stage of life your dog is going through. To know what stage of life your dog is going through, of course, you would have to know his age. The main stages that dogs go through are the **impressionable** stage, the **adolescence** stage, the **adult** stage, and the **senior** stage.

The **Impressionable** stage (also known as the critical socialization period) occurs around the ages of eight weeks to five months old. In this stage, you will find that your puppy is very excited and

curious about life. The things that happen to him in this part of his life, whether they be positive or negative, will stick with him for a long time. And it is possible for some things to last a lifetime. The bad things that usually happen to dogs in this stage of life are not done purposely. They are usually mistakes that the owner did not mean to make; for example, when toy dogs get their toes stepped on. When you are cooking in the kitchen, and you are really into what you are cooking, and you do not remember that you have a dog. I have seen many pet owners step on their dog to the point of breaking their dog's toe. If this happens to your dog, he might feel uncomfortable walking with you. That can lead to leash walking issues. Negative situations can also occur with the doors in your

home. **You have to remember that you have a dog.** When closing the door, you want to make sure that your puppy is

nowhere near the door when it closes. Tell your family members to watch behind themselves when closing any of the doors. Sometimes when children get upset, they run to their rooms and slam the door as hard as they can. That behavior needs to come to a stop immediately. If you are downstairs getting ready to leave, and you think that the puppy is upstairs, still close the door gently. Your dog's head or neck could get slammed in the door. I have seen that happen to a few dogs after which the dog puts on the brakes every time his owner tries to walk him out of a door. Many dogs get hurt because of this behavior, and I have even seen some dogs die right on the scene, as well. The number one thing that you do not want to have happen in this stage or in any stage of your dog's life is that your dog gets bit by another dog. That can cause a change in your dog's attitude for an extremely long time and maybe a lifetime. If your dog is experiencing the impressionable stage of his life right now, I'm so excited you found out about this book at this early stage of your dog's life! This stage right here, I would say, is one of the most important parts of a dog's life, if not the most important. Reading this book at this stage of your dog's life will really set a strong foundation for your dog. It will teach him to work for what he wants; have fun working and pleasing you; and it will keep him stress free. If trained properly, this stage of the dog's life can help him out throughout all of the other stages he will experience.

The **adolescence** stage occurs around five months to two years old. This stage is similar to the teenage years for children. You have a teenager now. Just like a teenager, your dog will be obstinate, very testy, and sometimes, he just will not listen to you and takes what you are saying as a joke. Like a teenager, your dog

 has an adult body for whatever breed you have, but they just do not have that adult maturity yet— just like a teenager. Your dog is maturing and going through changes. They are

going through sexual maturity, which usually kicks in around six to eight months. If your dog is not fixed, the females will go into season (heat) and start spotting all over your house for three weeks once every six months. The males in this stage will start lifting a hind leg and mark their territory; for example, your house plants, the corners of your walls, the legs to your kitchen table, and maybe even you. They are also going through behavioral maturity and will eventually calm down. This usually kicks in around one to two years; for some dogs, it may take three years. This is sometimes the case with Retrievers. They are also going through changes—physical, mental, and emotional changes. All of these changes are really stressful for the dog, and when they have an owner that does not really know how to raise a dog, the dog is even more stressed out. So, that is another reason why I am glad you are reading this book. You will learn the right things to do when raising your dog no matter what stage of life he is currently experiencing.

The **adult** stage (also known as the social maturity stage) of a dog's life is two years to six years. At this time of the  dog's life, he is no longer acting like a big baby. He has calmed down a little. If you are starting training with an adult dog, there is good news and bad news. Well the good news, as I said earlier, is that your dog has calmed down a little since he is an adult now. But the bad news is that the older the dog, the more patience you must have in training him (that is if he is not already trained). Now your dog is stronger. Whatever problem behaviors he has, can take a long time to curtail. You are going to have to be very patient.

The **senior** stage occurs over seven years of age. "Can you teach old dogs new tricks?" Yes, you can. But like I said earlier; the older the dog the more patient you are going to have to be.

Question

I know that you can tell a dogs age by looking at his teeth, but how do you compare dog years to human years?

Good question. Yes, you can tell a dogs age by looking at his teeth. Many people still think that each human year is equal to seven dog years. Studies now show that a dog's first year is equal to fifteen human years; the second year is ten more human years; and every year after that is like three human years.

Now, before we get started with training, there are a few tips I want to give you that will help you succeed with training your dog. (1) Dogs—they are a lot like children, but guess what? They are not children. I know that is hard for some pet owners out there to hear. But if you start training your dog thinking that he is your little baby, you are not going to get very far with training him. And he will probably end up running the house. (2) Dogs will be dogs. So that means you need to treat them like one. It does not matter how well trained your dog is. Sometimes your dog will mess up. We humans mess up too. Do not get so excited when he does wrong. Always be calm and stay on top of any bad behavior. Try to notice the good more than you notice the bad. (3) If you do not want to be a stressed out pet owner, there are three components you *must* have. YOU HAVE TO HAVE **PATIENCE, CONSISTENCY,** AND YOU HAVE TO **PRACTICE.** If you do not have even one of these three things, you are going to find yourself getting very stressed out. (4) There are three things on the dog's part that has to be right for you to succeed in training your pet. These three components are: **NUTRITION, *EXERCISE*,** and **HEALTH.** If your dog is lacking in any of these three areas, training him will be difficult. When following these tips while training your dog, it will make your experience stress-free. We will talk about these three things later in the book.

My philosophy on dogs that have never been trained is this. To have the perfect dog, it takes time and proper technique. You might ask, "When does this training time stop?" From experience of training different breeds of different ages, I think it depends on how old your dog is. I feel that dogs under two years old should be on a strict training schedule until they reach two years old. Dogs that are two years and older should have at least three months of intense training. Following this training period, you can finally sit back and enjoy your life. Remember that some things should always go on like No Free Lunch. We will talk about No Free Lunch in chapter two.

Let's talk about your house. Most of the bad behaviors in your dog are due to the manner in which your house is organized... Dogs learn these problem behaviors from somewhere, and it is usually the way the house is set up why they learn to destroy things. You want to teach everybody in the house how to **CONTROL THE ENVIRONMENT.** This is very important to do. The following are a few examples of how to **CONTROL THE ENVIRONMENT:** keeping the bathroom garbage low or empty. Without reading a dog book, I am sure you know that dogs like to shred papers. I am also sure that your dog has shredded something in your house already. I have been in some homes where the dog had taken the roll of toilet paper while it was still attached to the wall and made a mess all over the house by running with the tissue in his mouth. Another example of controlling the environment would be to keep the regular garbage cans in the house and the dirty clothes hamper from overflowing. Do not have the garbage can in your kitchen overflowing with zesty trash such as chicken bones. If your dog accomplishes stealing some of the overflowing trash, he just got rewarded. If that keeps happening, it is possible that your dog will turn into a garbage thief. The hamper is equal to the garbage can. The hamper should not be overflowing with dirty laundry. The socks you have not worn yet that you just bought do not taste good to most dogs. But the socks you have on right now that you were playing football in, the socks used when exercising, and the socks you wore during your four to eight hour shift at work taste very good to your dog. So make sure when you are separating the laundry that he is not there to help you. Rewards do not only come from you. Milk bones are not the only rewards to a dog. Rewards to a dog can be your attention (eye contact, talking, and your physical touch) when you come home. Rewards can be many different things. Dogs will be dogs, and they will have their problems. You just want to try your best so that your dog does not have all the problem behaviors that are out there to have. Pearl, my Rottie, has a problem with socks. If she is loose and sees a dirty sock available, she will destroy it. Again I say each dog has his or her problem. It is also important to keep your coffee table clear of any ashtrays or tissues. If you have a computer that has many cords in the back, it is a good idea to zip-tie them together. I want to share one other example of how to control your dog's environment. When you come home from the grocery store, you can no longer put the bag of groceries on the floor beside the kitchen table or the island. It is best that you put the groceries directly on the island or on the kitchen table.

Let's talk about your dog being food motivated. If your dog is motivated by food, you are in luck. When a dog loves treats, it makes dog training an easier experience. I am not saying that dogs that do not like treats cannot be trained, but it is sometimes hard. It takes a lot of patience. Later on in this book, I will go over what to do with a dog that is not motivated by food. When giving your dog or puppy treats, you want to make sure you do not spoil his appetite. One way not to spoil his appetite is by treating him with bite-size treats. A treat can either be a meal (the whole treat) or a taste (a small piece of treat), and you want it to be a taste. Large treats can allow dogs to chew too long and have the owner lose a dog's attention. Dogs should get a taste of what they like when they do something you want. Most treat packages are going to say that the treats are bite size. What may be bite- size for a large dog (for example a Labrador) may be a meal for a small dog (for example a Yorkie). Make things easy for yourself. Buy soft treats. With soft treats you can break the treat as small as you want, and the dog does not take too long to eat the treat, and there are no crumbs left on the floor afterwards. I have to admit, the treats I use are not all that soft, but they are soft enough. For the ten years that

I have been training dogs, I have always used freeze dried liver treats. There are some dogs that like these liver treats, but their stool becomes too soft. If that happens to your dog, use different treats. These treats work wonders. Dogs love them!

When giving your dog a command the right way, there are four steps you have to go through.

1. **Attention**
2. **Command**
3. **Reward**
4. **Release**

I see many owners when they tell their dogs to sit; the word comes out there mouth about five to fifteen times before their dog finally sits. Most owners when telling their dogs to sit do not have the dog's attention. In a little while, we will go over how to get your dog's attention. When you have your dog's attention, you can tell him to do whatever you know he knows to do. When your dog does the behavior you want him to do, you must praise him right away—"Good boy or Good girl!" Something to remember--there is one more step after praising your dog. You want to be the one to release him. After you praise him, waste no time, go straight to the release word. Most owners clap their knees when releasing their dog. Their release words are usually "OK!" Very few owner say "BREAK! " DONE!" or "FREE DOG!"

Let us focus now on getting your dog's attention. Most pet owners go straight to giving the dog the command, when giving their dog a command to do. They just do not understand why the dog is not responding. Most owners end up saying the command about five to fifteen times before their dog does what he was told. That should not be. When you give a command, you should only have to say it one time. In the ten-minute activity that we are about to do, this is the only time in your dog's life that he will get treats just for looking at you.

Getting Your Dog's Attention

Get your treats out! If you can have a friend or family member participating, it will make things easier. You and your friend should be face-to-face and at least three feet away from each other. The person getting the attention should have the leash. Have your bite-size treats out. Have the person without treats distract the dog. Now try getting the dog's attention back. If saying his name does not work, say your dog's name at the same time as touching his nose with your treat. Not your finger but the treat. Right after touching his nose with the treat, bring the treat up to your nose. As soon as you get his attention, reward him right away-- *the quicker the treat, the quicker the response.* You may sometimes notice that your dog is responding way too slow when you give a command; this sometimes happens with the sit command. You tell your dog to sit, and then he starts wobbling back and forth, then turns in circles, takes a few steps back and then finally sits. To fix all of that, try giving the treat as soon as he completes the command. Get his attention ten times the right way, and make sure you're tapping your dog's nose with the treat and not your finger. After doing this about ten times the right way, throw in a distraction. Have the person distracting the dog use a squeaky toy to do this. Do it this way about ten times as well. You might start noticing that your dog is starting to associate hearing the squeak of the toy with looking at you and getting a treat. That means you did not even have to say his name, and he looked at you.

Notice that good behavior. That is very good if your dog does that. If he will look at you without you

saying his name, he will be more than happy to look at you when you do call his name. When doing this attention exercise, the last three of the ten that you do try to just say his name without tapping his nose with a treat, but give a treat when he looks at you. Make sure your dog swallows the treat before getting his attention again. Something you might not have noticed is that dogs lick their nose every time they swallow something.

If your dog is not food motivated, there is another way. To get your dogs attention, blow on the back of his head or firmly poke his rib with your finger. Just make sure you say his name while you do that.

Homework

Doing the above exercise should help your dog pay attention to you much better. When getting your dog's attention on a daily basis, it's best not to use too many treats. Associate his name with things that are good; for example, meals at meal time, your coming home from work or school, when calling your dog to come to you, etc. Try not to associate his name with anything that is negative. Make sure no one in your home gives the dog any treats for him giving eye contact any more.

Massage

It is imperative that you touch your dog daily to get him used to being touched on the uncomfortable parts of his body. Some call this nursing your dog. After being told from your veterinarian that your dog is in good health, start massaging your dog. Now that you know your dog is in good shape and health, as you massage him, take a mental note of how your dog's body is supposed to feel. And if it is ever different in the future, notify your vet. As I coach you through this, scrutinize the part of your dog's body that I talk about. (1) Start the massage with the back legs. Pick a leg or both and thoroughly massage it. The most important part of the legs is the foot. Softly pinch in between each toe. If your dog is not trying to bite you, notice the good behavior, but if your dog does bite you just say the words "No" or "No Bite" in a firm voice and then continue touching him again. If he does not stop the biting, take a break and continue the massage when your dog calms down. (2) When you are done with the legs, do the tail next. Gently pull on it; that is, if your dog has one. (3) Now rub your dog's back and try working your way to your dog's shoulder blade. While you are rubbing your dog's back, do not just rub in the direction of your dog's coat only, but in both directions. While rubbing in the opposite direction of the coat, now you can check and see if your dog has any fleas or ticks. If he does have any fleas, it will look like somebody poured black pepper on your dog's skin. I will go over flea and tick control later. (4) Now you are up to the shoulder blades and the two front legs. The front legs are more important than the back legs. Why? The front legs have two important parts. These two parts are the under arms and, of course, the feet. When touching his underarms, try to lift him up to where his two front feet are not touching the ground. (5) Now try working your way up your dog's neck and to the ears. You will find that your dog is very comfortable with having his ears touched. In fact, he is probably going to love when you massage his ears. But the part that might be tough to do, or that you might not want to do is sniffing your dog's ears. It is important that you know the right way that your dog's ears are supposed to smell. I am not saying that the ears are going to smell like cologne or

perfume, but you just need to know the difference between a good

dog smell and a bad dog smell. If it is ever a bad dog smell, believe

me, you will know. That bad smell will probably mean that your

dog has an ear infection. (6) The last part of your dog's body to

work on is the face. Massage the forehead, in between the eyes,

and then the muzzle. You have done well, but, just so you know,

there is one more part of the head. Open your dog's mouth, and get

use to touching in side of his mouth. Touch the tongue, the teeth,

and the gums. In the future, if or when your vet says to give your

dog a pill that is not chewable, you will not have a problem

opening your dog's mouth and feeding him that pill. Just so you

know when giving your dog a pill that is not chewable, it is good

to coat the pill with peanut butter or rap it in cheese, and give it to

your dog as if it were a regular treat. Doing this, your dog will not

even chew it; he will just swallow it. When your dog licks his nose

after swallowing the pill, it is always good to rub his neck

underneath his chin in a downward motion. This will help the pill go down easily. Touching inside of your dog's mouth will also help when you decide to brush your dog's teeth. It is important to massage your dog daily. You should also massage him before and after you board him at a kennel; and you should also do this before and after a play date with another dog. Dogs are not as wimpy as us humans. They can get cut and walk like everything is normal until you touch it. I have even seen where some dogs after getting hit by a car; they get right back up and continue walking.

Allow me to explain to you why it is good to touch these parts of your dog's body. When touching your dog's feet and calmly praising him at the same time, you are preparing him for future nail clippings; whether it is from you, a groomer, or a vet. With all of these parts being touched, you will prepare your dog for groomers, vets, and children that will be touching your dog in the near future. Why is the tail important to touch? The tail is one of the most important parts of the body for the dog to be comfortable when getting touched there. Misunderstandings (dog bites) can occur when your dog is not okay with having his tail touched. These bites usually happen when young children are not being supervised. The child approaches the dog from behind without the dog knowing, tries to catch the dog in order to stop the wagging tail; and the dog without checking to see who it is behind him, reacts by quickly turning around, with his mouth already open, to defend himself. And now that child may need stitches because of this misunderstanding. Now this dog is probably going to be labeled as a "Biter", or might even get put down, when this dog may really be an angel. Most owners that do not know much about dogs—in a situation like this one—will get rid of their dogs. Situations like this sometimes bring tears to my eyes. If you are thinking of getting rid of a dog just because of this one incident, seek advice from a professional trainer. The dog's biting may have been a misunderstanding. It is not a good idea to adopt a dog just because you saw one on television. If you do not know anything about dogs nor plan on doing research on the dog you want to adopt, a dog is probably not the kind of pet for you. If the dog is accustomed to having his tail touched, more than likely he will just turn around with his mouth closed or panting, possibly knocking the child over from excitement. Be careful when touching underneath a dog's arms. Some dogs do not like to be picked up by their underarms. There have been cases where children have had to get plastic surgery done to their face because they touched a dog by his underarms. The bigger your dog is the more you should try to de-sensitize him to being touched there. Let's say that one day your child comes home from a good day at school, and he cannot wait to say hello to the family dog. Your child sees the dog and runs up to him to give the dog a hug. Your child now picks the dog up from underneath his arms. If your dog is not used to that, he will react violently. When a dog is getting hugged like that, both the child and the dog's face are close together. This closeness can make the dog feel restrained. Remember that dogs will be dogs. If at any moment they feel uncomfortable or restrained, most dogs will react by biting. You must always supervise your dog and children when they are together.

Homework

Congratulations for completing week one. Week one has much information to take in. This chapter has many things that are really good to know and explains how to quickly put them into effect. Take it easy this week. You do not need to do too much with your dog this week. Make sure you and your family members have a meeting. The following topics should be discussed in the meeting: Controlling the environment, boundaries / limitations for the dog, daily routine for the dog, supervising the dog, and exercise. If you do not control where and when the dog releases his energy, he may release it in your house. Start massaging your dog daily. The feet should be touched more than once a day. Do it every time you and your dog are watching television together. For this week, just do those simple things and I will talk to you next week. Remember! Next week; same time same place. Rain or shine make sure you are on time.   Enjoy.

CHAPTER 2

(Week 2)

Welcome back. I am happy to see that you did not give up on your dog. Remember the key to successful dog training is **patience, practice, and consistency.** If everything went well with your understanding of the last chapter, this next part should be easy. I want to quiz you on some important things that were mentioned last week. If you do not score a hundred, re-read chapter one until you fully understand.

Quiz # 1

1. If your dog is one year old, what stage of life is he going through?

2. If your dog is three months old, what stage of life is he going through?

3. In order, what are the four steps with giving your dog a command?

4. What three things are the key to successful training?

5. How do you make a dog respond faster to commands?

6. When other than daily should you massage your dog?

7. Give an example of controlling your environment.

8. What parts of a dog's body can become uncomfortable to them as they grow up?

9. Should you give your dog a treat every time he looks at you when you call his name?

10. How should you work on teaching your dog his name?

Answers
1. Adolescence
2. Impressionable or critical socialization period
3. Attention, Command, Reward, and Release
4. Patience, Practice, and Consistency
5. Give him a treat as soon as he responds to a command.
6. Before and after you take your dog to the kennel; Before and after play sessions with other dogs
7. Not having the garbage overflowing with trash
8. The paws, tail, and under the arms
9. No
10. Associate his names with things that are good

I hope everything went well with your quiz. As you progress in training, there will be more quizzes on things that are important for you to know. I think you will enjoy what we discuss this week. I would like to go over with you solutions for any of your dog's behavioral issues and more. This whole chapter should be read at least twice. You are probably going to find yourself coming back to this chapter for helpful tips in the future. In this chapter, we will be going over how to correct jumping, how to stop excessive barking, how to stop mouthing on you or furniture, and how to stop digging. Know that all dogs will do most of these things, but that does not necessarily mean that your dog is doing something wrong. Some dogs will jump on you if they have not seen you for a few days and then the jumping quickly stops because the dog knows how to control his energy. If that is the case, jumping is not a problem with your dog. Some dogs will bark to let you know that someone is approaching the house, and then stop when you notice that person. That kind of barking is not a problem. Some dogs will gently grab your hand with their mouth to bring you somewhere. They might be trying to show you something. This does not mean your dog has a problem with mouthing. When it is hot outside, most dogs will dig until they get some cool dirt to lie on. If your dog does that, good news for you, your dog does not have any issues with digging.

Confine your dog for little while, clear your mind, sit down, relax, and let's go over some solutions for the problematic behaviors of your dog.

Biting

If you have a puppy that is only a few months old, I am guessing that your main problem is the puppy nipping. If your dog is an adult and still has a problem with biting, that behavior is called mouthing. The first thing that you should know when dealing with puppy nipping or mouthing is that you are not going to stop a dog from chewing. They need to chew, but you can control what they chew on. Is your dog between the ages of three to five months old? If so, I feel your pain. I know what you are going through. I like to call that three to five month stage of puppy nipping "The Pac man stage". They literally go around the house chomping on anything they can get their little mouths on. They chew on things such as the corners of your walls, your plants, your banisters, your antique wood table, the legs to your futon, you, and more. If you cannot supervise a dog that has unruly behaviors in the house, he should be confined. We will talk more about confinement in chapter three. When you catch your dog in the act of destroying your house, you can correct him and show him the right thing to chew on. When you catch him in the act, you can shout out "No, Hey, or Ehh-ehh". Just make sure you are not shouting out his name in order to correct him. You do not want him to associate his name with things that are bad. As soon as your dog switches over to the right behavior, you should switch over to praising him. After any kind of correction, you have to praise your dog right away. Praising your dog should always be at least double the amount of time that it took to correct him; for example, when you catch your dog in the act of chewing on one of your socks - let's say it takes you three seconds to stop your dog. When your dog stops, you should give at least six seconds of praise.

Puppy nipping can sometimes be difficult to get through. A few things that are important to know about this issue are *that dogs cannot bypass this stage in their life, you can get through it the right way, or you can make the biting problem worse.* Most pet owners end up making it worse. But lucky you, I am going to help you with getting through it the right way. Now that you know there is no way to bypass puppy nipping, this knowledge should help you out with not being too firm with your dog.

I know that many pet owners go to their vets for advice on puppy nipping. I want to make this very easy for you to understand. Going to your vet for pet training advice is not always a good idea. Vets are there to make sure your puppy or dog is in good medical shape. Dog trainers are specialist in dog behavior, and veterinarians are medical specialist. It is best to get tips on dog behavior from a reputable trainer. My saying this does not mean that I am speaking poorly of vets. Please do not get me wrong! Most of my referrals come from vets. I have many friends who are vets. Many pet owners while at the animal hospital, ask their vet for some training advice. That is not a problem. The problem occurs if the vet is not sure of how to answer the question but they answer it anyway. Now the same thing goes for us dog trainers that are asked medical questions from our clients. We really have no right coming to any conclusions about your dog's health; that is a vet's job.

Let's continue. Remember you do not want to be too firm when your puppy bites. I am going to tell you the right and the wrong way to get through mouthing or puppy nipping. It is imperative to keep your dog occupied with a chew toy. First I want to start with the right way. Dogs tend to bite when you are petting them. A good solution is Bitter Apple or Bitter Yuck. These two items are deterrents because dogs do not usually like the taste. You can apply either solution to your arms and feet to stop your dog from nipping you. If your dog starts licking off the no bite spray from you, this is not the solution for you. Some dogs actually like the taste of that stuff. Do not apply the spray if you have any open cuts. Another solution that I will share with you is clear unscented deodorant. You can apply that to the parts of your body that your dog bites. If that doesn't work, then try the solution that I find works with most dogs, peanut butter. You can put small amounts of peanut butter on your wrist and on your ankles. Have you ever seen a dog eat peanut butter? You are probably going to laugh when you see this! When a dog sees that you have peanut butter on you, all that they can do is lick you. A dog licking you is better than a dog biting you.

Unknowingly, most pet owners are making this puppy nipping stage even worse. Be careful when wearing shirts or sweaters with long, loose sleeves. If your dog starts tugging on your clothes, do not show a friend and start laughing about it together. You are just stimulating the dog, and will produce more biting. Dog owners sometimes like to play slap boxing with their dog. This activity is a lot of fun, but if your dog still has a biting problem, it will aggravate the problem. Do not have tug toys visible if you have a dog that bites. Put them away until he has overcome his biting problem. The stringy ends of rope toys are very similar to the ends of the rugs in your home. These types of toys must be removed temporarily.

Digging

If your dog has a problem with digging, the solution is different for inside and outside the house. And, of course, with any problem that you are having, try to find out why or how it started. If or when your dog digs inside the house, you have to be there to catch it. When you are not there, your dog should not be there either. If your dog has unruly behaviors in your house, he should be confined when left alone. We will talk more about the proper way to confine a dog in chapter three. If you are supervising when your dog is loose around the house, digging should not be a hard problem to fix. This behavior usually occurs when the dog sees a piece of the carpet sticking out. If you lock him in a room with carpet, he will try to dig his way out. You do not want to set up a booby trap for digging problems in your house. It is better for you to catch your dog in the act. When you catch him, shout out, "Stop, Hey, or Enough", while clapping. You can also correct him by using a spray bottle or a shaker can. Make sure the spray bottle has only water inside. The shaker-can should have coins or pebbles inside. Make sure that your dog does not associate the correction with you but the shaker can. It is always better to try out the spray bottle first. Only do this if you catch your dog in the act. After your dog listens to your correction, you have to remember to praise him. Remember you have to be *consistent*.

When dealing with a digging problem outside, it might be hard to catch your dog in the act. Remember that dogs will be dogs and dig up some cool dirt if it is too hot outside. If this is the reason why he is digging, he is not trying to start any trouble. Correcting a dog to stop digging in this situation can possibly jeopardize his life. Do not worry, there is a solution. Because your dog is overheating, he digs. If your dog has a lot of fur, you might have to cut it down some. Tell your groomer about your situation, and ask them to give your dog a healthy cut. If your dog does not have a long coat and digging for the same reason, keep him in a shaded area, or just do not keep him outside much. Now if the digging issue is not because of his getting overheated, the best thing to do in this case is set up some kind of booby trap. Now just because I say "set up a booby trap", it does not necessarily mean that it is something that is going hurt the dog. When setting up a booby trap, you do not want your dog to see you set it up. Some dogs might know you are up to something. What I am going to tell you is painless to your dog. One solution is poop. Yes, you heard me right. You could use your dog's own poop. Put the poop in the hole that your dog made. Lightly refill this hole up with dirt. You actually want your dog to go back to that same spot and dig. But now when he digs, he will be digging up his own mess. He will not like that, and will then go to his next main digging spot. And if you set up the same trap for all of his digging spots, digging is going to no longer be a fun task for him. This will work with most dogs. Notice that I said "most" and not "all". The reason why this solution might not work for all dogs is that some dogs have what they call *carprophagia* – eating their own stool. You can also put a piece of chicken fence in that spot and bury that back over lightly too. That should work as well. Dogs do not like grinding their nails on that fence at all. This solution—chicken fence- is great for dogs that dig in your garden since you may not want dog poop in your garden. You should be able to find this at your local home improvement store. You can put this around your garden. You can stand the chicken fence up if you want to. Most owners do not like to do so. They believe it will lower the value of their property. What you can do is lay it on the ground around your garden. This will protect your garden from your dog and many any other animals that might wander onto your property. All of these solutions should work within a few days.

Barking

Before you try to control your dog's barking issues, you need to figure out what kind of barking your dog is doing. With most barking issues, barking is just the symptom and not the problem. There are five different types of barking – boredom, learned, fearful alarm, dominance-territorial, and excited play alert barking. It is important to know which one of these factors is stimulating the dogs barking for the simple reason that the solutions vary based on what is causing or motivating the dog to bark.

How do you know when your dog is barking out of boredom? How do you fix it? If your dog is barking for long periods of time, and you are receiving letters of complaints in the mail without a return address, these are usually signs of your dog barking out of boredom. When you are dealing with this kind of barking, barking is not the problem. Barking is just the symptom. The problem is more than likely boredom. Are you giving your dog sufficient exercise? If you feel that he is given the right amount of exercise and the barking continues, then your dog is in need of more exercise. Is there anything that you can do for the dog when you are not home? In a situation like this, proper exercise is critical (later on in the book, we will discuss proper exercise). It is good to have a toy to keep your dog occupied. A good chew toy in this situation is a toy like Kong Toys, Nylabone®, or Hollow Bones. Patience, consistency, and proper technique are three things that you need when dealing with problems like these.

Excited play alert barking occurs when your dog sees something that he wants but cannot get to it. These may include squirrels, other dogs, deer, cats, cars, etc. This type of barking can happen when your dog is in the house or when out for his walk. You will probably notice your dog doing the play bow or bouncing all over the place. When doing this, your dog's face will be relaxed. His ears will be back, and his hackles will not be up. Find out what is exiting your dog and desensitize him to that stimulus. You should do some "sit –stay" exercises in those areas. Make sure you are not making the problem worse by encouraging small animal chases, soothing your dog when he barks, etc. You should only soothe or praise your dog when he is not barking at things that normally distract him. In this case too, the barking is not the problem. It is just the symptom. Your dog is just very excitable. The "stay" command will help reduce his energy level.

Fearful alarm barking can sometimes be surprisingly easy to fix. This type of barking comes from dogs that are either under socialized or genetically shy. You might notice that your dog's ears go back, eyes dilate, hackles are up, and his tail is between his back legs; you might also notice your dog leaning on or hiding behind you. Make note that the barking is not the problem. Again, it is just the symptom. Your dog is afraid, and that is the problem. Find out what your dog is fearful of and then help him develop a *threshold of tolerance*. <u>A threshold of tolerance is the distance away from the distraction to the point where your dog is calmed.</u> This distance is different with all dogs. For some, it can be ten, thirty, fifty, or a hundred feet away to develop the threshold of tolerance. When you feel your dog is getting comfortable with that distance, work your way closer to the distraction. After a while, this will allow your dog to tolerate the distraction being near him. I find that most fearful dogs are usually sensitive to water or sound. If your dog is sensitive to water, you can use a water bottle. Shoot a stream squirt towards his muzzle. You can also use a shaker can, too. Be careful with this tool because you can really startle your dog. You need to know the level of sound that works with your dog. All you are trying to do with these tools is redirect your dog's attention. When your dog barks or growls at the distraction, you do not want to use too much force like hitting your dog or yanking the leash. If you do that, your dog may develop fearful aggression. Then your dog will try to attack whatever he is afraid of before it can get near him. Remember--to succeed at getting rid of an issue like this, you need to have time, patience, and proper technique. If you decide to go to a trainer to get extra help, you might want to consider one-on-one private training instead of group classes.

Dominance territorial barking can sometimes be hard to resolve. The name of this barking problem adequately explains itself. It's when dogs bark at everything that passes by your property, or they bark at people while on walks in their neighborhood. In many cases, owners like when their dogs alert them when someone is around, but the barking becomes too much after a while. This problem is common with working security breeds such as: Akitas, Rottweilers, German Shepherds, and Doberman Pinchers. The key to this is control. When you find out why your dog is barking, you want to be able to say "quiet", and your dog stops within seconds. If your dog is having this kind of barking problem when going for walks, you should stop him from marking his territory. If you live in an apartment and cannot let your dog eliminate in a yard of your own, pick one spot and one spot only that your dog can mark. Check and see if your dog is water or sound sensitive. When your dog barks, firmly say, "Quiet!" and wait about two seconds. If that does not work, try it again while using a shaker can or squirt bottle. When your dog is quiet for about two seconds, praise him. You never want to soothe or hit your dog when he barks. If you do that, you might stimulate the behavior and possibly make your dog aggressive. Dogs with this problem need to get sufficient exercise-wearing your dog out to where he cannot make another step. Barking dogs should get at *least* a three-mile walk *daily* unless you allow him to run around in a fenced in yard. If you feel that all of these solutions are not working, as a last resort, you can use a remote trainer (shock collar) or a citronella collar. Please consult with a professional trainer before doing this. If your dog is not getting proper exercise, do not expect these solutions to work. If you are having this type of barking problem, there is a question you need to ask yourself. "Is my dog dominating me?" When you try to correct your dog, does he bark at you? If yes, get in touch with a reputable trainer to help you. You should do private training in a case like that. This will all work out with patience, time, and proper technique.

Learned barking is very common with all types of dogs, big and small. This type of barking occurs if your dog wants something from you or wants you to do something; for example, barking to get food at the dinner table; barking to come out of the crate; and barking to get your attention. You should give your dog an alternate behavior to do for him to get what he wants. He should sit for what he wants and not wine at the same time. If you train your dog to quietly ask for what he wants, you have to make sure to notice his good behavior. That is important. It is also important to not give any attention to the barking. If you give attention to it, *you* will make it happen even more. One other thing that is good to do also, is to allow your dog to do an *extension burst* which allows your dog to bark and bark to see how long it takes him to stop on his own. You have to make sure to give him some praise when the barking stops. With some dogs the extension burst can continue for hours. The longest extension burst I have ever heard lasted six hours! These are the solutions for barking problems that your dog may have or develop. Remember, with some barking issues, it can take a while to curtail. This problem is not something that goes away with time but with time and proper technique. If you give your dog sufficient amount of exercise, his bad barking behavior will go away quicker.

Jumping

Jumping is a common problem that many owners have with their dog. Why? When dogs jump up on their owners, most owners either do not care, or they try their best to give a big correction to the dog, but the dog sees that big correction as a big reward. And remember, whatever you reward your dog for will cause them to repeat the same behavior. So you want to make sure you are really giving a correction and not a reward. Usually the correction for a jumping problem is negative punishment. Negative punishment is when you take away a reward from a dog to correct his bad behavior. Your dog must also know how to sit for this jumping to go away (we will talk about "Sit" after jumping). First you need to know why your dogs are jumping. Yes, it is for your attention. They want your eye contact, verbal communication, or physical touch. If you use any of these three things to correct a dog, your dog will find it rewarding; for example, you stare, yell, or knee your dog, and the dog may find that very rewarding. By instinct, dogs will jump when mom or dad comes home. When a mother wolf goes hunting for food for her puppies, she does not come back with shopping bags. The groceries are all in her stomach. The puppies know by instinct to lick the mother's mouth and she will regurgitate the food and then they can eat. I hope that does not happen to you when they lick you on the mouth, but this is what they are really looking for when they jump on you. Your goal should be to have your dog sit and greet you when you come home. Pet your dog while he is sitting. When dealing with a jumping problem, be aware of these three factors: *friends and family, strangers, and the house*. In many dog books, you will find many solutions for jumping. However, I will give you fewer solutions that will actually work if you follow them correctly.

Make sure all visitors that come over know that your dog is in training. Keep the leash on the front door knob when you are expecting visitors. Your dog should be leashed when visitors come over. Leash your dog when doing this until you feel he is calm around visitors. Something else to remember is to help and allow your dog to do things on his or her own. When visitors come in the house, there should be some treats nearby that they can hold on to. I would like to repeat that visitors should know beforehand or upon arrival that your dog is going through training. If they do not want to cooperate, the dog should be confined (we will talking about crates in chapter three). Those that will cooperate instruct them not to interact with the dog unless the dog sits for them. Then it is okay for them to reward the dog with a treat. If the dog jumps, you want to correct him by saying "Off!" Guide the leash down when you do this. It is very important to reinforce good behavior from your dog as he greets and interacts with your visitor. If your dog is quietly sitting when you and your guest converse, then give the dog what he wants—eye contact, verbal communication, and physical touch.

Now let's talk about you (the family). When you or your children come home from work or school, you need to do the same exact thing every single time. While your dog is in training to eliminate jumping when you enter the house, have treats handy as you enter the home. If you cannot find treats that work for your dog, try out freeze-dried liver treats. The children should have treats in their book bag. Your situation when you come home might be that your dog has had free run of the house; your dog may be confined to the kitchen; or your dog might have been confined to his crate. When you come home, have about three to five treats handy. When you approach your dog, have the hand with the treat down to your dog's mouth. Allow your dog to lick your hand and put him at arms distance. Do not wave the treat in the air. If you do, your dog might use your body as a ladder to get the treat. When you feel that your dog's attention is now on the treat and not on you, command your dog to sit. But when he sits do not give him the treat yet. When your dog sits, get down to his level and pet him while he licks the treat in your hand. Release the bite-sized treat after fifteen to thirty seconds. As your dog is eating that treat, quickly take out the next treat and do the same thing with rest of those treats. Studies show that it takes the average dog two to three minutes to calm down when you come home from a day's work. If you are sure that you are following the solution correctly and it is not working for about five minutes, stop what you are doing, go in your room without your dog, change from your work clothes, come back out, and try it all over again. Please do not get to the point where you start feeling bad for your dog- to the point that if he takes too long to catch on, you give up, feel bad for him, and give him attention even though he did not earn your attention. That is giving too much affection. The more free affection you give a dog, the more he will walk all over you. Two weeks of proper training should produce good results. This is tough—let's say there are four people in your house, and three of you are doing exactly what you are supposed to do; however,   the other person is still trying to train the dog to jump on command. The other three might as well give up on what they are doing if that one family member does not stop!

Saying hello to strangers can sometimes be a little difficult. You need to be in control of your dog and of the person that you are allowing him to say hello to. The reason why most owners do not have control over that stranger or their dog is that they are not sure or confident of what to do. You can usually tell that a person wants to pet your dog from about ten feet away. Tell that person to hold on "My dog is going through training. Please wait for me to put him into a sit before you pet him." Have your dog sit on either side of you facing the stranger. Try not to have your dog sit in front of you with his back turned towards the stranger. When your dog sits, hold him down by the collar. During or after the stranger pets your dog, hand your dog a treat and praise him. At first you are forcing your dog to greet strangers the right way by holding the collar down, but after a while your dog will start doing it on his own. Notice the good behavior when your dog starts to do it on his own.

When training your dog not to jump on furniture in the house, there are a few things that can really help you out. Scat mats, plastic carpet protectors, four-foot leash, double sided tape, and some cardboard—believe it or not these tools can actually help stop your dog from jumping on furniture in the house. Jumping on couches, kitchen counters, stoves, and tables, are all examples of dog jumping in a house.

Both scat mats and carpet protectors can help prevent your dog from jumping on your couch. Lying a scat mat down will give your dog's paws a mild-static shock. This solution should work out for you, but for some dog owners the scat mat is much too expensive. Well, I want to tell you a cheaper way. Carpet protectors flipped upside down will also work. With the sharp plastic studs sticking up, that will make it uncomfortable for your dog when he jumps on the couch. Carpet protectors are not expensive. Scat mats and carpet protectors are especially good for dogs that have free run of the house when you are gone.

A four-foot leash is another device used on dogs that are not yet left alone. Allow your dog to drag the leash around the house while supervising him. When your dog jumps on something, calmly approach him without any screaming, grab the leash, and gently guide him down while telling your dog "off". As soon as all four paws are on the floor, praise him right away. After a while, all you will have to do is touch the leash and say "OFF!" A while after that, all that will be needed, is the word "OFF". When you are not able to supervise your dog, he should be confined.

Double-sided tape can work to prevent dog jumping on counter tops. Put the double-sided tape around all ends of the counter. Dogs do not like the sticky feeling on their paws. If you are worried about the double-sided tape leaving a mess when you take it off your counter, you can put the double-sided tape on some card board.

SIT

Teaching your dog to sit is one of the best ways of teaching your dog to have good manners. The technique is always the same for introducing any position to a dog. It is always best to lure your dog into the position without forcing him. While doing this, "Sit"

should only be said one time. As soon as your dog's bottom touches the floor, say "Sit" nicely, sharply, and firmly.

Immediately give a treat after you say "Sit". When luring your dog into this position, it's best for you to be on his level. Properly lure your dog into this position about ten to twelve times. Now let's go ahead and stand up and give the dog the sit command. Your dog should now be ready for the signal. If you do not have a signal for your dog, use a flat palm toward the ceiling. This signal works well. When you give the signal, do not have your hand too close to your dog's face. Keep your hand extended in front of your chest. Make sure everyone in the home uses the same hand and signal. When giving a signal, have only one treat handy.

Sit is a control behavior position. It does not mean that you have total control when your dog sits, but you do have some kind of control. At all times, no matter where you are, you want to at least have some kind of control over your dog. Everywhere you go with your dog make sure that he will sit for you. It should not matter where you are; what time of the day should not matter either. Your dog should sit 100 percent of the time.

Homework for Sit

Making sit into a reliable command all depends on how well you do your homework. Read this part carefully. This is one of the

most important things that will be said in this book. It is important that your dog be put on a strict **No Free Lunch** policy. This means no free reward at all (not talking about treats) unless your dog earns it by doing something for you. You are probably wondering what I am talking about when I say rewards. Rewards

in the environment should not be given freely. The following are a few examples of rewards: opening the crate door, feeding meals, opening the

house door (to go eliminate), greeting you, and much more. I

suggest that everybody in the household have the dog follow the

No Free Lunch policy. This is a lifetime policy.

Chew Toys

The proper chew toy is a toy that is not consumable, unless

it is an edible chew or treat. Chew toys are important for your dog,

as they satisfy the dog's natural urge to chew and help prevent

boredom and   destructive

chewing   behavior.

Be sure to   choose

the right   chew toy,

based on the   size of your

dog and its chew   strength. Nylabone®,

for example, makes great chew toys. They use high quality

materials and offer chew toys for dogs of all sizes. For really

strong, aggressive chewers, look for Nylabone Dura Chews® or

Durable chews. For average chewers, Nylabone makes a Flexi

Chew® or Flexible chew. Nylabone®, also make chews just for puppies!

Another good toy is the Kong toy. I like to call them doggy pacifiers. This is my favorite toy. Not for me, of course, but for my dogs. These toys have a weird shape. When playing fetch, the dogs have much fun. The dogs do not know where it is going to land, and they race all over the place trying to catch it. The best part about this toy is the hole in the middle. You can put all types of small treats in it. Most pet owners put some peanut butter in their dog's Kong toy. If you have never seen a dog eat peanut butter before, you do not know what you are missing. Only put a spoonful of peanut butter into the Kong toy. If your dog shows no interest in the toy, I will let you in on a secret. You can fill the Kong toy with chicken or beef broth and freeze it. Simply, smear some peanut butter or cream cheese over the small whole of the Kong toy and place it in a cup with the large hole facing up. Then fill the Kong toy with broth and freeze it. Your dog will love this long lasting, flavorful taste.

Stuffed animals are good, too. Not the ones you win at the carnival, but the ones you buy from your local pet store. If you feel that the stuffed animals are starting to promote destructive chewing behavior, do not give them to your dog. When you give your dog the correct stuffed animal as a chew toy, do not throw it away after your dog has destroyed it a little. The first thing that dogs go for are the squeaky. When your dog rips a hole into the stuffed animal, help him get all the stuffing out. After you are done, give the skin of the stuffed animal back to your dog. It is better for your dog to rip that to shreds instead of your shirt for work or your socks. Some pet stores sell stuffed animals for dogs without the stuffing inside.

It is important to stay away from hard bones that eventually get soft and break easy. Well, just like I am with all of my clients, I am going to be real with you. Bones that eventually get soft are just bad news. These type of bones dogs chew and suck on, but when it gets soft they try to swallow it. This is not safe. I have only seen a few dogs chew on this chew toy responsibly.

Most dogs end up having to get surgery because these soft bones sometimes get caught in their intestines. Bones like compressed rawhide that break into many pieces when swallowed are okay to give a dog to chew on. Supervise your dog before leaving him alone with any new toys.

Collars

It is important that you know the simple things there are to know about collars. Here are some commonly asked questions about collars.

- How do I know if my dog's collar is the right size? Two fingers—you should be able to put two fingers in an upright position comfortably when touching your dog's collar. Two fingers up and down, not sideways.

- Should my dog have a buckle or clip collar? It depends on what kind of dog you have. If you have a toy dog, it does not really matter what kind you use. For dogs that are medium size and up, it is best to use a buckle collar. These dogs tend to pull a lot more. If a little piece of that plastic clip collar breaks, your dog can break loose. If that happens in the wrong place, your dog can get seriously hurt.

- I am sure that my dog's collar is the right size, but he still gets out of his collar. What do I do about that?   There are certain collars for dogs that like to escape. It is called a "Martin Gale" also known as a "Greyhound" collars. These are no-slip collars. They make it more difficult for a dog to slip out. You will know that you have the right size if it goes on one ear at a time and comes off one ear at a time.

- My dog pulls way too much, and I feel I do not have any control when he does. Should I get a choke or a prong collar?   Your dog might not need anything. You always want to know that you are giving the proper correction with the collar that you currently have your dog on before you plan on upgrading collars. First seek professional help on

how to correct a dog. If the problem still occurs,

then it is all right to upgrade.

When attaching a leash to your dog's collar, make sure you

do not attach it to the "rabies" tag. I have seen many pet

owners make this mistake, and they are confused as to why

their dog got loose. If your dog ever gets loose because of

collar breaking, you want to know how to turn the leash

into a collar and leash. This is very easy to do. Put the clip

of the leash through the loop of the leash. This will turn the

leash into a collar, too. After making a collar out of the

leash, put it on your dog and pull up on the clip.

HOMEWORK

It is nice to see that you have completed week 2

(Chapter 2). This chapter contained much information, for

these are things you really need to know. Start putting the

solutions for those problem behaviors into effect.

Remember that it can take a while for those problems to curtail. Just make sure that you are taking care of them the right way. Before you come to the conclusion that your dog has a few behaviors that need to be fixed, make sure you are doing your part. This means giving your dog sufficient exercise. This week you also want to start putting the No Free Lunch policy into effect. Make sure your dog has the correct collar on, and if it is a puppy that you have, make sure you check the size of his collar weekly.

CHAPTER 3

(Week 3)

As always, it is good to have you back again, and it is good to know that you did not give up on my book or on training your dog. By now I think you know my style. I like to open the chapter with a quiz on important things to remember from last week.

Quiz # 2

1. What are three important things to know about the puppy nipping stage?

2. True/False: It is okay to leave your dog alone with a toy when you first get it for him.

3. True/False: When setting up a booby trap for your dog's digging problem outside, you should allow him to see you set it up.

4. Can giving your dog proper exercise curtail a problem that he might be having?

5. What is the best way to check and see if your dog's collar is the right size?

6. How do you introduce a new position to a dog?

7. Is "Sit" a control behavior position?

8. How would you work on "Sit" for homework to make this command work reliably elsewhere?

9. What does "No Free Lunch" mean?

10. Give three examples of "No Free Lunch".

Answers:

1. Three things to know about the puppy nipping stage is that you cannot bypass this stage of a puppy's life, you can get through it the right way, or you can make things much worse.
2. False
3. False
4. Yes
5. If you can stick two fingers vertically in your dog's collar comfortably, then your dog's collar is the right size.
6. Lure your dog into the desired position without saying a word until the dog hits the position. When they hit the position, say the word one time as you are giving a treat.
7. Yes

8. You want to work on Sit at home all day by doing No Free Lunch.
9. No Free Lunch means giving your dog no free rewards (not talking about treats) unless he earns it and does something for you first.
10. Three examples of No Free Lunch are making a dog sit for things such as: opening his crate door, putting his meal down, and for greeting.

I hope everything went well with Quiz # 2. Do not be afraid to highlight the areas that you feel you will need to review later on. This book is yours. Do what you have to do to make yourself comfortable with the techniques.

Okay. Now you are up to week three. Do not worry. This week is not as hard to take in as were weeks one and two. From this point, things get a little easier. This week I would like to talk about safely introducing your dog to other dogs. I want to explain the importance of dog crates; the "Drop it" and "Leave it" command; introduce the "Down" command; and also to touch on leash walking.

Saying hello for the first time

It is very important to have your dog say hello to an unfamiliar dog in the right way when doing so for the first time. Most owners ask each other if it is all right for the dogs to say hello and will usually question each other by asking each other their names and addresses. Some even go as far as setting up play dates for their dogs. The pet owners are doing all of this while the dogs are nose to nose. This closeness can become dangerous. Keep an eye on the dogs. We never went over this before, but I still want to ask you a question.

Question

Exactly how long do you think your dog will remain safe going nose to nose with another dog that he has never met before?

A. 30 seconds

B. 1 minute

C. 2 seconds

D. 10 seconds

If you answered C, that is correct. If the two dogs do not

know each other, to be on the safe side, it is best that they go nose

to nose for only

two seconds before

they are gently

separated. When

you separate your

dog from the other

dog, gently reel

your dog back to you. If you yank the leash while separating the

dogs, you will possibly generate aggression in your dog towards

the other dog. When saying "hello" to another dog, the owners

should not even look at each other, let alone hold a conversation.

Make sure the dogs do not get tangled in each other's leash.

Remember, if your dog gets bit by another dog, that occurrence can stick with him for a long time, even a lifetime. Training your dog to be comfortable around other dogs can take a long time depending upon how well you work at it.

There is more to saying hello to another dog than knowing how long to keep the dogs together. You also need to judge by looks if it is feasible to even say hello to the other dog. Before you allow your dog to say hello to another dog, make sure that the other dog's body language, leash, and collar are acceptable.

Be aware of the other dog's body language before saying hello. Use discretion before saying hello. If you think that the other dog is showing signs of dominance or aggression in his posture, do not say hello. The chest out, the dog's head held high, hackles up, tail up wagging stiffly—these are all examples of dog's dominant or aggressive posture. A dog that is showing relaxed behavior will have a leveled head, ears will be back and relaxed, hackles will not be up, and his tail will be wagging lightly. Make sure that both dogs are showing relaxed behavior before they say hello.

If either of the dogs has on a retractable leash, just say "no" to saying hello. If the two dogs get tangled with the retractable leash, this alone can be dangerous because of the cords. Just the other day, I was walking my Yorkie with a retractable leash, and I was holding the lower part of the leash with my hands. I gently yanked the leash to correct her for walking too fast, and I cut the side of my finger open. If that can happen to me while correcting my nine pound dog, just imagine what can happen if two dogs get tangled in a leash like that.

If you are not sure about the other dog's behavior and his collar is too loose, walk away. I have seen dogs get loose when saying hello, and sometimes the ending was not good. You do not have to put your fingers in the other dog's collar to make sure of this. You should be able to tell by looking at the dog.

Dog Crates

Do you have a crate for your dog? Do you know what size crate you need? Is your dog's crate located in the correct room of your house? Do you know when to confine your dog? And how long should your dog be in the crate? Crates are good to have when raising an energetic puppy, while housebreaking, and when correcting unruly behavior in the house. Playpens are also good to use for time outs. Some owners think that dog crates are cruelty to animals. They feel that the crate is hurting them because the dog is whining, barking and crying. Well, if that is the case, take your dog outside of the crate and give him a massage and see if you can find any weak spots or cuts. I'm very sure that you are not going to find anything wrong with your dog.

You also want to make sure that you have the correct size crate for your dog. What size dog do you have? Is your dog small, medium, large, or extra large? Some examples of small breed dogs are Chihuahuas, Yorkshire terriers, and Maltese. Examples of medium breed dogs are Beagles, Jack Russell, and Cocker Spaniels. Examples of large breed dogs are Rottweilers, Retrievers, and German Shepherds. Examples of extra large dog breeds are Newfoundlands, Saint Bernards, and Great Danes. If you have a small breed dog, use a 24"crate. If you have a medium breed dog, use a 36". If you have a large breed dog, use a 42". If you have an extra large breed dog, use a 48". Notice that I said the size of your breed and not the size of your dog. If you purchase a crate for a large breed puppy for the size he is when he is young, you are probably going to end up purchasing more than one crate for your dog in the near future. Make sure you get the size crate that will comfortably fit your dog for a lifetime. There is also a way to know if your dog's crate is the right size by just looking at it. Your dog should be able to stand up comfortably without hitting his head on the top of the crate. He should also be able to turn around comfortably without rubbing his face on the sides of the crate.

It is important that your dog's crate be located in a certain part of your house. You want to be able to confine him and still make him feel like a part of the family. When confined, they should be able to see and hear what is going on in the house. Put the crate in the highest traffic area of your home – the most activity. The following are examples of high-traffic areas in your home: the foyer, the kitchen, the family room, the master bedroom, and the basement. You should only put the crate in the basement if the basement is finished.

It is imperative for the safety of your dog and your house that your dog is crated at the correct times. If you have a puppy or an adult dog that has unruly behaviors in the house, crate him every time you cannot supervise him. Many pet owners think that the only time their dog is without supervision is when they are not at home. There are times when you are in the house that you cannot watch them. Very few pet owners I know allow their dogs in the shower with them. Therefore, during times like this, the dog should be confined. You may even work from home but you want to be alone. Confine your dog. Your dog should only be loose around the house when you can watch everything that he is doing. If you leave one room in the house to go to another, your dog should be right behind you. If you are trying to experiment by allowing your dog to roam the house on his own, make sure you can hear where he is. Put bells on your dog, or if your dog has rabies and an ID tag on, that should be enough for you to hear him. When you can hear your dog, that is good thing, but if you cannot hear him, quickly check on him. Clients ask me all the time, "When will I be able to allow my dog to have free run of the house?" This is not like a child where you would give him more privileges as he gets older. It depends on your dog's level of training. If it feels like your dog is on that level, it is up to you to allow your dog to have free run of the house. It is best to gradually allow your dog more freedom around the house. The following behaviors should no longer exist when allowing your dog more freedom: house breaking, destructive behaviors, and excessive barking. Your dog should also have love for all the other animals in the house before giving him the free run of the house. I highly recommend not giving him total freedom until the dog is at least a year and a half years old. Dogs that are in the adolescence stage—even if they seem trustworthy enough to be free around the house should not be trusted yet. This is that stage where most dogs surprise you---the stage where your dog does something you never would have thought your dog would do.

Drop It

Training your dog to drop something is not too difficult. Remember when you teach your dog new things, always see that you are helping your dog and not doing for your dog. You are not training your dog when you pry his mouth open when he put something in his mouth. Life would be a little easier if you can just say to your dog "Drop it", and he opens his mouth and he drops it all on his own. This is possible! The trick to this is actually the same as with the "Watch me" command, but two things are different. Whatever is in your hand needs to be twice as good as what is in your dog's mouth. And, of course, you will say "drop it".

Question

I have a Yorkie, a toy dog, which loves to grab things and run underneath the bed where I cannot reach him. What do I do if I cannot reach my dog?

Well, the answer to that is actually very simple. If this happens often, allow your dog to roam the house with a leash attached to him. When working with your dog in the house, a four-foot leash is the

best kind to use. When he has a leash on, make sure you supervise him. When he is underneath the bed, you should be able to see his leash sticking out. Reel him out and get the item back.

Question

What do I do when my dog grabs something and starts doing the house-race-track thing with it in his mouth?

Well, most dogs have their owners trained because the owners are just running around the house with them. If they are running around the house with an item they should not have in their mouth, stand where you are with something better in your hand than what he has in his mouth. Wave him down as he passes you. You might miss him the first time. Just make sure you do not give up. After a while he should stop and drop the item. Remember that the quicker you give the treat to your dog, the quicker he will respond.

Leave it

There are a few different ways you can teach your dog to leave things alone before he picks them up. Remember to remain calm in all situations. Do not freak out when your dog is about to put something in his mouth. Just calmly correct him and move on. You are lucky if your dog is sensitive to water because you can use a spray water bottle. If your dog is

motivated by food, this next solution should work for you. Hide a few of your dog's best treats where he can smell them but not get to them; for example, hiding the treats under your hands or your feet. When you hide the treats make sure you have a treat in your other hand to give him when the command is completed. I usually hide the treats underneath my foot. When your dog tries to get those treats, he is going to scratch and lick your foot. After he stops and looks at you, firmly say "leave it". If your dog does not leave it after a few seconds firmly say, "Leave it" again. Keep doing this until he leaves the hidden treats alone. As soon as he leaves it, you need to treat him right away.

Another way of working on the "Leave It" command is to surround him with his favorite items around the house. Yes, this means allowing him to wonder around a room with shoes, socks, tissues, ash trays and more placed on the floor. As he wonders around the room, you should have by your side either a spray bottle, shaker can, or a leash attached to your dog. When he gets too close to the item, firmly use what you have to correct him. Remember that you want to praise your dog right after any kind of correction.

Down

Remember that the procedure for "Down" is the same for teaching all positions. Lure your dog into the position without saying a word until your dog hits the desired position. By now your dog knows how to sit already. So you can just say the word and give the signal to your dog. After your dog sits, put the treat to his nose and slowly lure his nose straight down to the floor. After your dog sits and you put the treats to his nose to lure him down, they usually jump to your hand to try and get the treat. To avoid that, quickly put the treat to his nose after he sits. Never go ahead of his nose on this command. Once your dog's elbows have both touched the floor, treat your

dog while saying the word "Down". Try your best to allow your dog to do this on his own. Never push your dog into the down position. Again, let him do it on his own. If you are introducing this command the right way, it will still take a while to hit the "down" position for some dogs. You want to be patient when teaching this command. Just know that the first attempt to doing the "down" position is usually the hardest one. After completing the first down, your dog will catch on to what you are doing very quickly.

Homework for the down

Take about five to ten minutes out of your day to do the exercise shown above. When you work on the "Down" command, use treats. If you feel your dog is really catching on to what he is doing, you do not have to give him a treat for every down that he does. You should also mix the down with no free lunch. When giving your dog his meal, make him do down instead of sit. No longer should your dog sit for meals. For all that food, the least that your dog can do for you is the down position. Soon we will make him sit and stay for his meals. But for right now just make him go down.

Loose leash walking

Many of you probably could not wait for me to touch on the topic of leash walking. Allow me to fill you in on something. Please pay close attention to what I'm about to say, for it is very important. Out of all my years of training dogs, I have realized and found out that most training for the dog or human comes while going for walks. Training for you or your dog can come from walking. If you are walking your dog on the leash the right way, you can gain that overall control that you have been looking for. Now the same thing goes for your dog too. If they are taking you for a walk the right way, they can dominate you and gain that control over you that they may be looking for. Dominant dogs come in all different sizes. When going for a walk, you should not

be walking with your dog. Your dog should be walking with you.
The leash walking that I want to talk to you about is not going to
be the perfect heel exercise. Heel is the leash walking that you
want to achieve when walking your dog. I will be going over how
to "Heel" with your dog in a future video that I have coming out
soon. In this book, I just want to show you the best way to get your
dog's attention while walking him on a loose leash. The type of
leash walking we will be going over is *loose leash walking*. When
you master this type of leash walking, your dog will stop all that
annoying pulling, and he will learn how to keep an eye on you
when walking. You will gain much control by doing this, but not
as much as you will during the heel exercise.

Activity

When doing this exercise, it is best to do it with a six-foot
leash. Let's first go over the rules for this type of walking. 1) Keep
your dog on your left side, but not necessarily right by your side.
They can be all the way in front of you or all the way behind you.
As long as they are on your left side, they are all right. 2) Do not

walk at your dog's pace or stop for your dog. Now that I have given you the rules, I want to tell you the technique. Do this exercise in an open area such as your front or back yard or at a park. Now set your dog into a heel sit. This means making your dog's right shoulder blade parallel to your left leg while being in a sit. With your left hand holding the lower part of the leash make sure your dog is in the heel sit properly. The loop of the leash should be in your right hand. When you are all set to walk, say to your dog "Let's go". When you start walking, let the lower part of the leash go out of your left hand. Now you should just be holding the loop of the leash. Make sure you are walking at your pace. Right before your dog pulls you, make a sharp u-turn to your right, and keep walking. Before you turn, give your dog a verbal indication first. You can say, "Turn, this way, or the dog's name". If he does not turn with you, firmly guide him with the leash while turning around to walk the other way. Make sure you do not pull the leash when you turn. You just want to tug on the leash. Keep walking back and forth until your dog starts paying attention to you when you turn. When you get his attention, do one last turn and try your best to get him to land into a heel sit all on his own. This means you should not have to hold him back by your side with the leash to make him sit. Do whatever you have to do without holding the leash back. So this means you can say sit; tap his nose with a treat to get his attention; or you could give him the sit signal to help him do it on his own. Remember the whole point of this exercise is to get your dog's attention.

Question

What if I have a smaller dog that does not like to walk on a leash at all?

Dogs that are not used to leash walking may take a little longer to train. These Dogs are usually being picked up too much. First you have to get your dog used to being on a leash. The best way to do that is by letting him roam the house with a leash attached to him. Make sure the leash is not too thick or heavy.

Whenever your dog has a leash on while wondering around the house, make sure that he is being supervised. Because he is all right with having the leash on him, does not mean that he is going to walk perfect for you. He still may drag behind a little bit. When your dog does that, just keep walking. Once he starts taking just a few steps on his own, stop walking and praise him for doing so. And keep adding on distance that he is walking on his own and, of course, praise him for it. If this problem is happening with a smaller dog, it might make things easier if you walk him on a harness.

It is okay to do loose leash walking when you go for your daily walk with your dog. It is very simple. If you want to add your own rules, that is all right. But the main rule is that it should feel as if you are not even holding a dog at the other end of the leash. So this means it is okay for your dog to walk where ever he wants, but if you want him to walk by your side that is all right, too. <u>The main idea is that he should be able to stay inside the circle on his own</u>

while doing whatever it is that he is doing. When your dog is fully trained to this kind of loose leash walking, distractions should not keep him from walking properly, nor will he pull outside of the circle. You should do loose leash walking in a serene environment where there are not too many distractions. And you should do a "heel" when walking through crowded areas with many distractions.

Homework for loose leash walking

Work on the loose leash walking that gets your dog's attention for at least ten to fifteen minutes in a day. This is a good exercise for the children to do too if you teach them how. When your children can walk the dog, it shows the dog that he and the child are not equal, and the child has a higher position in the household than he does. Remember to work on this in an open area such as your backyard or at the park. When doing this exercise, be firm to get the best results. Before you go for your daily walk with your dog, do the back and forth exercise of loose leash walking. When going for that daily walk, make your dog sit every twenty-five feet. Remember the reason why you are doing this exercise is to get your dog's undivided attention.

I am glad to see that you have finished another chapter of my book and I hope another week of training with your dog. To train a dog the right way, it takes time and proper technique. If you are reading this book carefully, things should be going well for you and your dog. Make sure you follow the homework exercises for all the things learned in the chapter. Make sure the crate you have is the correct size for your dog as an adult. When you come in contact with other dogs, you must be cautious. Remember the three things to watch out for before saying hello to that other dog. Before you go for your daily walk with your dog, make sure to do some of the loose leash walking exercises to get your dog's attention.

CHAPTER 4

(Week 4)

I hope that what you have read so far has been understandable and pleasant to read. Well, before we really get into this week's lesson, I would like to start you out with a quiz of some of the important things you should have noticed in chapter three.

Quiz # 3

1. What are the three main things to watch out for when letting your dog say hello to a dog he does not know?

2. True/False: I should yank the leash after my dog is done greeting another dog he does not know.

3. How long should you allow your dog to go nose to nose with another dog?

4. What type of room in your house should your dog's crate be in?

5. How can you tell if a dog's crate is the right size by just looking at it?

6. When should your dog be crated?

7. Is down a control behavior position?

8. With which example of No Free Lunch should your dog go down?

9. Can not having a crate be cruel to your dog? Explain.

10. True/False: Crates keep your dog and your house

safe.

Answers
1. When allowing your dog to say hello to a dog he does not know, watch for the other dog's body language; what kind of leash he is on; and judge if his collar is the right size.
2. False
3. Two seconds is a safe amount of time for two dogs that do not know each other to say hello.
4. Your dog's crate should be in the most high traffic area of the house.
5. The dog should be able to stand up comfortably without hitting his head on the ceiling of the crate, and should also be able to turn around without scraping his face on the side of the crate.
6. When you cannot supervise your dog, he should be crated.
7. Yes
8. You should give your dog the down command when giving him his meals.
9. Yes. If you do not have a crate with a dog that is unruly when in the house, he can get into something that can jeopardize his life.
10. True

I like week four of training. Why? Because I know that you are going to like it too. I would like to talk to you this week about the importance of the *Stay* and the *Recall* command. And also show you a quick and easy way to train your dog to do these commands. The key to both of these commands is to *set up your dog to succeed*. Having your dog know how to do both of these commands can one day save your dog's life. Know this information. Read what is being said carefully.

Stay

I recommend that you read the entire part for stay before you attempt this exercise with your dog.

Really quickly, I would like to go over what the command *Stay* means. When you tell your dog to stay, you want him to stay in the position that you left him in until you either get back to him or until you release him from afar. Once your dog knows how to stay it makes life go a little easier with having a dog in the family. When it is a nice sunny day and I have the top down on my convertible car, it feels good to know that my dogs are not going to jump out of my car if I have to get out for any given reason. It also feels good to put my dogs at the entrance of my kitchen and they stay there while I am sweeping. Wouldn't you like for your dog to sit and stay in the same position when something spills on the floor until the mess is cleaned up? Or what about when you are getting out of your car, and you want the dog to come too, but he does not have his leash on yet. It feels good if you do not have to hold the door steady with your knee while trying to reach your hand inside to find your dog and attach the leash. The *stay* command will also help when you weigh your dog at the vet's office. If your dog has acquired this skill, weighing him will be easier and less embarrassing for you. To be able to have your dog stay for you in all of these real life situations, do homework exercises repeatedly. *Stay* is a command that you also want to generalize with your dog. What I mean by this is that you must master doing these exercises in more than one location; for example, your house, your front and back yard, a park, and any other location where you know they allow dogs.

The 3D's

If you have never been introduced to the 3D's of training dogs, it will be my pleasure to let you know what they are. The three D's when training dogs are **duration, distraction, and distance.** I would advise you to only work on duration right now— just knowing how long your dog can stay for you. Right now, do not worry about putting your dog in a sit-stay while you are trying to see how far your dog will allow you to back away. And if your dog is new at staying for you, do not see if he will allow you to squeak or throw a toy without moving. All you want to do right now, if you are introducing this command, is to see how long your dog can do it. Once your dog starts showing a clear understanding of the *stay*, then it is a good time to start adding distractions and distance.

Activity

This week we will work on the *Sit -Stay*. As you already know, the signal for *sit* is a flat palm towards the ceiling and stay is a flat palm towards toward your dog. When you give the *stay* command, you should back up a few steps. If you just want to back up one step that is all right too. After backing away, you should be able to put your hand down. However long that you think your dog can stand there on his own, that is the amount of time you want to take before going back to him. When you get back to him, give him a treat while he is still sitting. If your dog decides to get up as you give him the treat, snatch it away and tell him to sit. Continue to give him the treat if or when he goes back into the *sit*. Most owners make their mistakes when they get back to their dog. As they come back to their dog, the dog gets up and is still rewarded. That is the incorrect way to do this exercise. Before your dog gets rewarded, he needs to sit and stay for you perfectly. This means you should be able to walk away and come back to him without his bottom moving. It is all right for your dog to look around as long as he does not move. He should not be able to move from where you left him and still be rewarded for it. Remember that whatever behavior a dog is rewarded for, they are more than likely to repeat the same behavior. So make sure the behavior you are treating is correct. If your dog was close to doing it the right way, you still should not give him a treat. Wait for the correct behavior.

Now that you have learned the right way to do the sit-stay, let us talk about how to introduce the sit -stay to your dog. We all know that the key to the *stay* command is to set your dog up to succeed. Believe it or not, I recommend that you make sure your dog fails the first time you try. Why? Because on the first *stay* that you do with him, he is probably going to fail anyway; and you want to know what you are working with before you force him to do it right. Once you say "Stay" and back away, most dogs will get up within half a second; some dogs a full second; and some dogs, five to ten seconds or more. You just want to see what you are working with. Starting with the second *stay*, you do not want him to fail any more. And if he does fail, *do not* treat him. Your goal is to make him stay longer and longer each time. Notice the good behavior as he does the sit-stay longer.

Homework for Sit-Stay

I would like to share a few tips with you so that the sit- stay will be mastered in no time. You should do this exercise in the same manner as the previous exercise. One of the best ways to work on the sit-stay exercises is by using the doorways. Yes, the doorways. You can do this using any door in the house. It can be your bathroom door or your bedroom door. The best doors to use though are the foyer (front) and the patio (back) door. This exercise is not too hard. An untrained dog will try his best to run right out of any opened door. This is why you should do these stay exercises at the door. When you do these exercises in the doorway, at first, you do not have to move at all. Just simply stand there with

your dog by your side. After you tell him to stay, fully open the door for a few seconds and then close it. Once you de-sensitize your dog to doors opening, go to the next step. This time tell him to stay as you open the door; step outside while your dog stays inside. Do not allow your dog to fail. If you feel he is about to fail, quickly go back and reward him. When you are done come back in, close the door, and reward him if he successfully completes the command. You can also work on this command with no free lunch. Only use the sit-stay with the situation of giving your dog his meals. I do this with my dogs all the time. I tell them to sit then stay as I walk a few feet away from them and set their food or water bowl down. After that, I walk away from the bowl, and then give them the command to dig in. Doing this will really help your dog with having better manners. Now when you feed your dog his meals, you should either make him sit-stay or go into a down position. Try getting him to sit and stay first. If that does not work out, give your dog the down command. By now your dog should be able to go down without a problem. Your dog at this time is going to be extremely happy to get food, but he needs to learn how to control all of that energy. If after five minutes the most, he does not accomplish the *stay*, make him do *down* to eat. You should never or rarely ever have to deprive him of a meal if you have been working on the down and the stay commands for homework the right way. If you ever have made your dog skip a meal because of the training process, do not feel bad. You will not hurt him by making him skip a meal. But you *do* want him to have access to water at all times, or for most parts of the day. For best results, it is good to give him his meals right after a nice long walk. Good luck!

Recall (Come)

Recall is another command that can save your dog's life. That is if he listens to you when you call him. Out of the 4,000 dogs that I have trained, only a few of them knew how to come back when their owner called them. And most of the dogs that did respond to this command had issues with being separated from their owners. These dogs naturally come to their owners, and did not have to be trained. "Why is it that out of the Sit, Down, Stay, and Recall commands that the recall seems to be the hardest one of all to train my dog?" This is a question that is asked of me all the time. The reason why in most households the dogs do not know how to come is simply that the owners do not want to take the time needed to train their dog to do so. When I go over the exercises for recall, you are going to feel that they are fairly simple. It is the required input time that is the hard part.

There are two rules with recall that are important to follow. 1) You always want to say your dog's name in front of the command. Instead of just saying, "Come", it is better to say, "Sparky come". Recall is a fun command for dogs to learn. Remember to associate their names with things that are good. Sit, down, and stay—if you already have your dog's attention, you do not need to say their name in front of these command. 2) This next rule is extremely important to follow when working on recall. You never want to correct your dog when he comes back to you on command. You might ask yourself "Why on earth would I correct my dog if he comes back when I call him?" Even though you ask that question, I'm sure somebody reading this book has done that before. Many owners correct their dogs when their dogs come back after they call them. I want you to take a good guess as to why most owners do this. Well, if you do not know I will tell you. Most pet owners call their dogs back only when the dogs are into something in which they should not be involved; for example, he is playing with a carcass; he is biting on the plants; or maybe he is digging in your neighbor's brand new garden. If you are dog smart, you should know that correcting during recall is not a smart thing to do at all. Recall is already one of the toughest commands to teach a dog. Spanking him when he comes will only make it harder to teach him recall. This comment leads me to my next statement - how to praise your dog when he comes back to you. When he comes back to you, you should give him a **jackpot**.

Jackpot is a fair amount of small treats given to your dog one at a time, or giving a lot of physical praise.

I know you are probably wondering why you cannot just give your dog the treats all at the same time. You can do that if you want to, but studies show that when you give that same quantity of treats to your dog one at a time, the dog sees it as a bigger reward. Again, your dog deserves a big reward when he comes back to you, and a jackpot is one of the best things for you to give him. Your dog may not take the treats, but he will not refuse physical and verbal praise.

Activity

One of the best ways to teach your dog the recall are the three steps that I am about to share with you. For this exercise you should get a training leash. Training leashes come in 6', 15', 20' and 30'. The longer the leash used is the better this exercise will work. *Do not use a retractable leash for this exercise.* You can hurt yourself if you use the retractable leash during this exercise. It is also more affective if you work on these exercises outside.

Step1) Allow your dog to wander off to where he is at the extent of the leash. When you feel that your dog has forgotten that you are there with him, say "(your dog's name) Come". You want to be firm when you say this command. Do not say it as if you are asking a question. As you call him, firmly reel him in at the same time. You want to help your dog to do this the right way. When he gets to you, give him his jackpot. Do these steps until you feel your dog has mastered it to where you no longer have to reel him in any more.

Step2) Now that you can trust your dog a little more you can now do the next step. Put his leash on the ground. Allow him to wander off again. And when you feel his mind is not on you, call him back. To make your dog respond quicker with the recall command, run backwards which will make him run to you faster. Remember to give lots of love when he comes back to you because he is now one step closer to doing it on his own. Do this step, until you feel comfortable that he is ready for the next one.

Step3) Make sure you spend an adequate amount of time on step two before you start step three. When you feel he is ready, take the leash off of your dog. Allow him to wander a little. Don't let him go farther than you allowed when he had on the training leash. It is always best to try calling him back when his attention is not on you. If or when your dog comes back to you, he will deserve all the praise in the world. This time he did the command all on his own. When working on step three, it is important to do so in a fenced in area. There have been owners who thought their dogs were ready for this step, walked along the roadside, let their dogs off the leash, and have never seen their dogs again. Therefore, do the third step in a fenced in area.

The recall command is a little easier and more affective to work on when someone is there to help you out. The two of you can make a game out the recall command. One of the games you can play is monkey in the middle. You and your helper walk away from each other and call the dog back and forth. If you have somebody to help you out, you can also play hide and go seek. To play this, have your friend hold your dog while you go hide behind something. You can hide behind a tree, a car, or a wall. When you call your dog, have your partner drop the leash so that your dog can find you. If you feel your dog knows this command just as well as he reliably knows the sit command, you may now try it in an unfenced area.

Question

What should I do if my dog gets loose, and he has not learned the recall command yet?

In any situation that happens when dealing with your dog, remember to be calm. It feels so tempting to run after him, but you should really do the opposite. Instead of running after him walk or run away from him. If your dog is in his impressionable stage, walking or running away will be fairly easy to make him come back. But if he is going through his adolescence or adult stage of life, you walking or running away from him might be difficult for your dog to come back. The only thing that you can really do is coax him into coming back to you. Make sure whatever you are using is more interesting than where your dog is or where he is about to go. There is something else much better than tricking your dog into coming back to you. And that is to train him to come back to you on command. After a while, he will have seen all the tricks you use to get him to come back to you. Usually when a dog gets loose and runs away, he is just trying to get much needed exercise to release excess energy. They must explore. This is something that *you* are supposed to do with him. Try not to walk the same route every single day. Sometimes switch to a different location. Later on in the book, I will talk about the proper exercise for a dog.

Note: There are some breeds that really should not be removed from the leash when they are in an unfenced area - breeds such as the Siberian husky and all hounds. Huskies are known for wandering off for miles. My uncle's all-white Siberian husky, Frisky, would run away for a few hours to a day. Later a police car would pull up at his home with Frisky in the back seat. The police would sometimes say that they had found Frisky over ten miles away. If you are a Husky owner, it is very important that you know that the breeds nickname is "Wonderer".

I want to briefly say something about hounds right now. There are two types of hounds, sight and scent. Neither type of hounds should ever be let loose without being fenced in. There are some hounds that you cannot adopt unless you have a fenced in area on your property. Because of their breeding characteristics, it is difficult to teach a reliable recall.

You always want to closely watch Boxers and Pugs when working on recall in hot weather. On a hot day, do not work on this command longer than a half hour. I have seen and heard of Boxers that have passed out while running around in the heat. These kinds of dogs do not breathe as easily as most dogs. Please be careful with breeds like these.

For better results when working on *recall*, work on it outside of your house. It is also good to use other treats that are better than the treats you normally use.

Homework for Recall

Now you know all the steps to take to teach the Recall to your dog. To have your dog reliably know this command depends on how well you do your homework. You should work on recall about half an hour to an hour. Some owners think that I am crazy when I tell them the amount of time that they should work on recall. They believe that they could never find that much time to give to a dog. I am really trying to be nice when I say this. If you cannot find at least half an hour to an hour to spend with your dog a day, you really should not have a dog. People that like animals but do not really have the time to spend with them usually adopt a cat, a bird, or a fish. The recall will be hard for some dogs to master, but if you carefully follow this method, it can be accomplished in approximately three months. This is a command you also want to generalize (master in different locations).

CHAPTER 5

(Week 5)

Hello, I am glad to see that you made it this far in reading my book, and I hope you also made it this far in training your dog as well. I am very sure you know what is coming up next. I have a quiz for you take. This is not a trap. These are just the top ten things of the last chapter that I really want to hit home. These are things I know you will be able to pass on to your friends and family who are also dog owners. Here goes Quiz # 4.

Quiz # 4

1. What are the three D's of dog training?

2. Why should you allow your dog to fail the first sit stay that you do when introducing it?

3. If someone else wants to start training the dog with the stay command, should they also make the dog fail the first one?

4. Should you generalize your dog to the stay command?

5. What does it mean to generalize a command?

6. Name a few locations that your dog should master when training him.

7. What two rules should you follow when doing the recall command?

8. How should you reward your dog after he comes when called?

9. How long should you work on the Recall exercises in a day?

10. When calling your dog to come to you, what can

you do to help your dog come faster to you?

Answers:
1. Distance, duration, and distraction
2. Most dogs usually fail the first one anyway. And you want to know what you are working with. Now when you do the second stay, you will know how long to wait before completing the command.
3. Yes
4. Yes
5. Master the command in different locations
6. Your house, your property, and many public locations
7. Say your dog's name in front of the command. And you never want to correct your dog when he comes back to you.
8. You should reward your dog with a jackpot.
9. At least a half an hour to an hour
10. Run backwards when the dog starts to come back.

This week I would like to talk to you about getting your

dog to go down for you without you having to get down with him.

I also want to go over the down-stay command. Your dog should

be at the point where we can start weaning him off the treats (fading the lure). I would also like to touch a little on the recall command again. And I feel it is important for you to know how to maintain your dog's appearance. So I will be going over the basic things you should know about grooming your dog.

The Goal for Down

I hope you have been working on the down command properly. This week, I want you to get to the point where your dog can go into the down position without you having to go down with him. You should be able stand up  straight and say or give the signal and your dog goes down. Before you start doing this exercise, keep in mind that the first down might take some time. You have to be patient when you do this. Good luck.

Activity

Note: Use your right hand when giving the down command.

To start this down command, make your dog sit in front of you. Make sure you are facing each other. After he sits, stand parallel to his right shoulder blade. Now, you and your dog should be side by side facing the opposite direction. Now, we both know that your dog can go down if you help him. Remember that we are trying to get him to do this all on his own. So make sure that you are standing straight up. Now is the time to give your dog the down signal, and keep it there. Make sure that your right arm is straight down when doing this. Have the treat in the hand that's giving the signal. Do not bend your elbow. When you do this, do not waste the word "down". Firmly say down when your dog's two elbows finally hit the floor. That is the only time you should say down. Be patient. The reason why you will have to be patient is that your dog will be taking a guess at what you want him to do. He does not know exactly what you want him to do. While your dog is trying to guess what you want him to do, he might do certain things--lick your hand, give you his paw, bark at you or jump on you. At some point, he will give up and just go down not really knowing that this is the response you desire. There is a way that you can tell when your dog is about to go down. When he is sitting there, you will notice him relax one of his back legs. And shortly after that he will go down. When your dog hits the down position, it is important that you reward him right away when his elbows touch the floor if you want this to work. After the first down, it gets much easier.

Homework

The homework for this way of doing the down command is the same as the homework for down in chapter three.

Down Stay

If the sit-stay is being mastered, the down- stay should not be too difficult. There is nothing different you need to know when doing the down-stay that you do not already know. One thing that I do want to remind you of is that the key to the *stay* command is to set your dog up to succeed.

No More Treats

You can only start weaning your dog off treats or correct him on a command when he starts to show a clear understanding of what you want him to do. What command right now do you think your dog has a clear understanding of? I would say the easiest command for your dog to do right at this point is "Sit". If you feel the same way, begin using this command with which to wean him off treats. Here goes a little training exercise showing how Mr. Springs weaned his dog Bella off treats for the sit command done in the correct way.

Mr. Springs and Bella: First Mr. Springs made Bella sit and treated her immediately. He released her then quickly tried to make her sit again but without a treat. As soon as Bella sat, Mr. Springs rewarded her right away with just physical and verbal praise. He even got her attention without using a treat. He released her and made her sit again using a treat. He then released her and commanded two sits from her. She got verbal and physical praise for those two sits. He released her and rewarded her with a treat next time she sat for him. Mr. Springs was almost done. Next, he commanded Bella to sit three times without giving her any treats. For the next and last sit he gave one treat and lots of love.

By showing the exercise with Mr. Springs and his dog, Bella, I hope you get a clear understanding of how to wean your dog off treats as he continues in training. Mr. Springs only got up to the point where he did not treat Bella three times. When training your dog, you can go more than that if you want. If you are using the *sit* command to first wean your dog off his treats, one location that should already be mastered is your house. Remember your dog should not get treats for sitting in the house because of the no free lunch policy. So the next location should be your property. I would say when you can get up to the point of giving a command twenty times without using a treat that you are ready to do this same exercise in a new location.

Grooming

I want to go over all the basic details about maintaining your dog so that he feels good and looks great. Let's first talk about how to keep your dog's coat looking good. Does your dog have a wiry coat like an Airedale? Is your dog's coat short and versatile like a Labrador retriever's or a Rottweiler's? Does your dog have a short coat without an undercoat like a Staffordshire Terrier? Instead of shedding, does your dog's coat grow long to where you would have to cut it like a Yorkshire terrier or a Maltese? Or is your dog's coat long and thick like a Husky or a German shepherd? Many new dog owners select a brush that is similar to ones used by humans. Some pet owners do not realize the type of brush used should depend on the type of dogs that they own. I have noticed that most pet owners have the double-sided brushes. With these brushes one side has soft bristles and the other side has wire bristles. However, if you have a dog with a wiry coat, you need to use a U blade on him.

If your dog's coat is short and thick, you should use a slicker brush, the furminator or a zoom groom brush. If you decide to use the furminator, you will not have to use anything else. With a dog that has a short coat without an undercoat you should also use a zoom groom brush. If your dog's coat does not shed but keeps growing, you probably need a double-sided brush, a slicker brush, or a rake brush. The main thing to worry about with a dog that has growing fur is that his coat does not get matted. The price at the groomers goes up if your dog's coat is matted. With dogs that have long thick coats, it is best to use the rake brush, the furminator, the slicker brush, or the zoom groom. Shedding cycles come twice a year during the spring and fall seasons. The first time a puppy will shed is between six and eight months of age. When it is shedding season, you should really brush your dog's coat daily. When it is not shedding season, just brush your dog's coat at least three times a week.

It is important that you do not bathe your dog daily. You should not even bathe him weekly! You will really dry out your dog's skin if you do that. The proper way to bathe your dog is once every four to six weeks. Let's say you wash your dog tonight, and it also rains tonight. And in the morning, he jumps off the porch and rolls around in the mud. Don't get agitated and wash him again. Firmly rubbing him with a wet towel can take care of that problem; or you can use baby wipes. Baby wipes work on any and everything. Or you can use pet wipes. If your dog rolls around in some poop or some carcass, then I would wash my dog again.

Ears

Next, let us talk about how to maintain your dog's ears. The procedure for cleaning a dog's ears is the same as that of cleaning a human's ears. You should only clean the parts that you can see. Do not try to stick a Q-tip down the ear canal trying to get the dirt that you cannot see. If you want to clean deep into the ear canal, consult with your vet first. You can injure your dog by doing that. Whatever you use to clean your dog's ears, whether it be a Q-tip, a cotton ball, or a rag, should be wet before you firmly apply it to your dog's ears. Remember to sniff your dog's ears daily to familiarize yourself with how a good ear smells. A change in smell might indicate an ear infection.

Just so you know, around the ears is a common place for ticks to hide. It takes a tick three to four days to effectively bite into you or your dog and draw out blood. After that, they will fall off. As you probably already know, there are some ticks that carry Lyme disease. The deer tick, the western black legged tick, and the lone star tick are all carriers of this disease. The best way to remove a tick is by using a tick spoon. Try to avoid walking your dog in areas with tall grass. Ticks do not only go on dogs. They go on humans, too. But if, for any reason, you do have to enter an area with tall grass, you should wear light colored long pants and long sleeved clothing. Now, if a tick gets on you, you will have a better chance of getting it off before it bites you. If you ever find a tick in you, take it out as soon as possible. It takes a tick up to twenty-four to forty-eight hours to give off the disease. If it is on you for more than two days, you should save it and get it tested to see if it was carrying Lyme disease. So remember to scrutinize your dog's ears daily.

Part of maintaining your dog's health is the treatment and control of tick and flea bites. Even though you cannot fully protect a dog from fleas and ticks 100% of the time does not mean that you should not try your best. One thing you can do is get a Lyme vaccination for your dog. You can also apply liquid drops to the back of your dog's neck to control flea or tick bites. I highly recommend FRONTLINE®, FRONTLINE® Plus, or K9 Advantix® for flea and tick control. Check with your vet for assistance with getting the right one. There is an important fact to know about K9 Advantix®. K9 Advantix® is for use on dogs only. But it is all right to apply FRONTLINE® or FRONTLINE® Plus on your dog and cat. It is best to get your dog's flea and tick control medicine from your local vet and not over- the -counter. Most things bought over-the-counter for flea and tick control are useless. Flea and tick solutions are sometimes applied incorrectly. Some pet owners make the mistake of applying the products a few hours before or after bathing their dog. For best results, it is best to apply this product two days after bathing your dog. You can also use flea and tick collars for control too. Just make sure that is not all you use if you live in a tick or flea-infested area. If after taking all the proper control measures you still find fleas and ticks, go to your local groomer or vet for further assistance. For more information on FRONTLINE®, please see www.FRONTLINE.com.

Nails

Having a dog that does not like to have his nails clipped can make your life rough. You do not want to need four people when clipping your dog's nails. It makes life easier when your dog willingly gives you or the groomer his paw while getting his nails clipped. When clipping a dog's nails, the same rules apply as if you are clipping your own nails. **Do not clip past the quick.** Why? The quick is a vein; veins carry blood. If you clip the quick, you are going to have some blood to clean up and bleeding to stop from your dog's paw. Professional groomers use kwik-stop or cornstarch powder if they accidentally cut a dog. If you do not have cornstarch powder, you can also use flour or baby powder. Apply as much as needed until the bleeding stops. If you are like me, you do not have the courage to clip your dog's toenails. I just send my dogs to the groomer to get their nails clipped. Remember to get your dogs used to having their nails touched. Touching your dog's nails should be a daily routine and more. Once your dog is okay with having his paws touched, you should work on getting him used to the clippers, too. Even if you do not know how to clip your dog's nails, I would advise that you still buy a pair of nail clippers. Open and close the clippers while touching your dog's paws with them. You can also get them comfortable with to having their nails touched by using a nail file. This will also help if your dog's nails are too sharp. Everyday file your dog's nails. Of course, the younger your dog is when you do this, the better. Notice any good behavior as your dog allows you to do this. It is best to clip a dog's nails once every other week. If you walk your dog on concrete on most of your walks, you are probably not going to have to clip their nails as much. If your dog is aggressive when having his nails clipped, let a professional groomer do it. Let them know the issues that you are having because they might have to muzzle him when clipping his nails. If they cannot do it, a good groomer will advise you to let a vet do it.

Teeth

Cleaning a dog's teeth is not as hard as you may think. The maintenance for a dog to have strong white healthy teeth is the same as it is for us humans. It is good to brush a dog's teeth after every meal. If you have a puppy that is under eighteen months of age, you do not need to use any toothpaste yet. Just use water in place of the toothpaste. Then when your dog's teeth actually need toothpaste, it should not be a big issue. Doggy toothpaste comes in beef, mint, liver, and peanut butter flavors. Make sure that you use a doggy toothbrush when brushing your dog's teeth. And for toy breeds, there are toothbrushes that you can slip right onto your finger to make things easier. It also helps if you allow your dog to chew on a good marrow bone. That helps your dog's teeth remain tartar free.

Homework

Make sure you keep working on your dog's sit and down stay. Make the near future a little easier for yourself and practice the down while you stand up straight. If you feel that your dog is starting to clearly understand his commands, start weaning him off his treats. Now that you know the proper way of maintaining your dog's good health, make a trip out to your local pet store and get the tools you need. Also, go to your vet and get any medication that you might need for flea and tick control. You do not want to forget how important it is to do the leash walking exercises. If you have children, and they want to walk the dog on a leash as well, make sure they work on the leash walking exercises as much as possible. Good luck!

CHAPTER 6

(Week 6)

Once again I just want to congratulate you for getting this far in dog training. I hope that you are reading this chapter because the previous chapters are going perfectly fine for you and your dog. To see if everything is going well from the previous chapter, take Quiz #5. The results will let you know if you should go back and read a little more of chapter five.

Quiz # 5

1. What is the goal that you want to reach when telling your dog to do the down command?

2. When giving a dog the down command while standing up straight, what will most dogs do to indicate that they are about to go down for you?

3. How do you know when you can start weaning a dog off his treats?

4. How often should you bathe a dog?

5. **True/False:** When cleaning a dog's ears, you should always try to clean deep down in the parts that you cannot see.

6. What disease do some ticks carry?

7. How long does it take a tick to do its job?

8. How often should you clip a dog's nails?

9. What are some things that you can use to stop the bleeding if you clip a dog's nail too short?

10. Are the rules the same with cleaning a dog's teeth like they are for humans?

Answers

1. I want to be able to stand up straight when I tell my dog the down command. I do not want to have to get down with him every time.
2. For most dogs they will relax their hips right before they go down.
3. When the dog shows you a clear understanding of what you are teaching him.
4. Once every four to six weeks.
5. False
6. Lyme Disease
7. Three to four days
8. Once every other week
9. Cornstarch powder, flour, or baby powder
10. Yes

In this last chapter, I am going to show you how dog food plays a role in a dog's training. I am going to touch some more on your dog getting loose and running off. One thing that I think you are going to like most about this chapter is that I will be going over the proper exercise that your dog needs in his life. I also would like to show you a trick to teach your dog that will actually help calm him down.

Nutrition

Keeping your dog on a good diet with the right kind of dog food, believe it or not, affects his training. Remember that the three key things that a pet owner must possess to successfully train their dogs are *patience, practice,* and *consistency.* There are also three key things the dog needs to have in order for him to have fun and for him to be trained successfully. These three things are *nutrition, exercise,* and *health.* If you and your dog have the three things needed for successful training, both of you are going to have much fun and become great partners. Right now, let us just talk about one thing at a time. Did you know that feeding a dog the wrong kind of food can cause hot spots, dry skin, or ear infections? Surprising, isn't it? If your dog has to deal with any one of these conditions, he will be much harder to train. It will be difficult to keep a dog's attention when dealing with any one of these issues.

Question

How do I know if I am feeding my dog the proper dog food? What brand should I feed my dog?

The correct person to ask is your vet. You want to feed your dog a good premium dog food. I have found out during my years of training dogs that people and dog food are almost like people and religion. Everybody has their own beliefs in the food that they think is the best to feed a dog. So the best person to ask is your vet. Do not rely on what individuals you might meet while selecting dog food to tell you what food is best for your dog. If you feel that your vet is just trying to sell you the dog food sold at his office, ask him to just let you know what things to watch out for when buying your own dog food. You may also research the proper dog food on your own.

Dry food vs. Wet food

Do you feed your dog wet or dry dog food? It is best to give more dry food than wet, if not all dry. Dogs need that crunch when they are eating their meals. Dry food will do that for them. If you do give your dog wet food, just make sure that you do not spoil him from eating dry food. Many toy breed owners just feed their dog's wet food. Wet food quickly dirties a dog's teeth. Dry food in a way actually helps keep a dog's teeth clean. Most pet parents give their dog's wet food mixed with the dry once a day at dinnertime. Make sure to check with your vet or breeder on how much food to put into each meal to keep your dog at the correct weight.

Dog food vs. Human food

Do you give your dog any human food? If you know what you are doing and know what human foods to cook, human food can actually be better than giving dog food to your dog. But if you do not know what you are doing with human food, and you are just experimenting with human foods, you should not give your dog any human foods. It is not good to give your dog any table scraps because doing so can cause health and behavioral issues. If you are not going to listening to my advice on not feeding your dog any table scraps, at least listen to me on the things you really want to stay away from when feeding your dog. **Chocolate, onions, raisins, and grapes**—these are some foods you should never give your dog. An overdose of these human foods will be toxic for your dog. And yes, hot dogs are terrible dog food. Just give it to them in small pieces if you use them as treats. Only use it for things that are hard to accomplish. The problem with hot dogs is that they are too salty. Fast foods like nuggets are much too salty for dogs to eat.

When you switch to a different dog food, there is a certain way that you need to do it. To avoid your dog getting a soft stool, switch the foods gradually. The safest way to do it is by the two-week program. During the first week, feed your dog 25% of the new food and 75% of the old food. On the first two to three days of the second week, feed your dog 25% of the old and 75% of the new. For the rest of the week, give him only the new food. If you do it this way, and your dog still gets diarrhea, you should feed him cooked rice. It can be yellow, brown, or white rice. It hardens up his stool right away. If you have fed your dog rice for three days straight and his stool is still soft, you should contact your local vet. His stool being soft might just be for another reason.

Your dog's meals should be given to him on a schedule. Giving your dog a feeding schedule, helps in more ways than one. It is almost impossible to house brake a dog if he does not have a schedule for his food. You should have a certain time that you put down and pick up his food. Put each meal down for about fifteen to twenty minutes. If your dog ever decides to run away, his feeding schedule will help out with that too. Most dogs when they run away come back home because they are either tired or hungry. Dogs live their lives on a routine like all other animals. Try to make sure that every day is similar. Keep him on a strict schedule. If you put his dinner down at 6:00pm every day, you should also pick it up at 6:20pm each day. When your dog knows his meal times, he will make sure that he does not do anything to miss it. Now if he runs away, he will try his best to make it back home for his food.

Question

My dog is not a big food lover. What if twenty minutes go by and he does not eat his food?

The rules still apply. If you know that there is nothing wrong with your dog, still pick his food up after twenty minutes. A healthy dog will not starve himself. Yes, you might go through a few dinner times without him eating, but he will eventually eat. But never deprive him of water. Your dog should be allowed water at all times. A dog will survive if he has to miss a meal. Remember only do this if your dog is in perfect health. Pickiness of food choices is usually an issue with smaller dogs. You can put broken pieces of milk bone treats in his food to help him eat.

Question

You say to allow my dog access to water all day. My dog loves water, and every time I put the water bowl down he drinks all the water. Should I still allow him access to that dish all day?

No, you really should supervise the amount of water your dog intakes. Give him some water mainly before going out to let him eliminate. If he seems thirsty, and it is not time for him to go eliminate, you can give him water but not a full bowl.

Puppy, Adult, or Senior food

You need to be sure that your dog is eating the right food for his age. A dog that is under a year old should be eating puppy food. Some large breed dogs need to switch over to adult as early as four to six months. Let your vet be the one to tell you the type of food your dog requires. Dogs that are between the ages of one to seven years old should be eating adult food. Dogs that are seven years old and up should be fed senior dog food.

Settle

The settle position is identical to the play dead position. Settle is the top control behavior position. Nothing shows you that you have total control over your dog like the settle position. When your dog is lying all the way on his side--this is the settle position. You can use this position as a trick or for behavioral issues too. When you play with your dog, does he sometimes growl at you, and you do not know if it was a serious growl or not? Since you know that dogs growl at other dogs, you feel that you can continue the play session. You begin to notice that your dog snarls at you when you are playing with him, however, you still continue the play. The situation will become a lot worse. Now your dog actually bites you, and this time it really hurts; or your dog bites a piece of your clothing and rips a hole in it. You become scared or upset, and you also realize that you have no control over your dog – **this is the time to do the "settle"**.

Many pet parents when taking their dog to the vet will ask the vet about behavioral issues concerning their  dog. Most vets will avoid recommending a professional trainer to their client but will themselves offer solutions for the problem. Most people and vets will tell you to put your dog into the settle position, but they will probably tell you to do it in a different way than how I am going to show you. Most people will say, "You have to be firm! Grab your dog's neck with both hands, and wrestle him down to the floor. Pin him down by his neck and hold him there until he stops moving. You want to show your dog that you are the Alpha pack leader." You do want to show your dog that you are the leader of the pack, but this is not the right way to do it with most dogs. It can be very dangerous if you take that advice and try to do the above-mentioned techniques to your dog. When you do those things to your dog—and that is if you win the battle-- most pet owners do not win that battle. Most dogs while they are lying there probably thinking to themselves that they just cannot wait for you to get off of them so that they can bite you even harder the next time. There is a way to wrestle a dog down to the floor, but if you are a first time dog owner or you do not have much experience with dogs, I advise you not to wrestle your dog down to the floor. There is a softer approach, and I would like to share it with you. Before I go over this softer approach, just know that some dogs are very uncomfortable with this position and may or may not hit this position.

Activity

Settle is the second step to the down position. First make sure that your dog is comfortable with going down. When dogs go down, they usually relax one of their right or left hips to the side. Some dogs have perfect posture and never relax. Whichever hip they relax on, you want to lure him to that side of their stomach.

Not to their hip but to their stomach. When your dog falls over on his side, say, "Settle" one time and give the treat at the same time. Most dogs are going to get up from that position at the same time you are giving them the treat. That is okay. If you want them to stay there for a longer time, when he hits the position, hold the treat in front of his mouth until you are ready to release him. You want your dog to go into this position as much as possible, on his own.

Homework

Well, as I have said before, to make something work in a real situation will depend on how well you work on it for homework. The best way to work on settle is to put your dog into this position while he is running around the house-race track. Make things easy for yourself when you do this. Use a treat. Good luck!

Proper Exercise

Giving your dog the proper exercise that he needs is a very important part of his training. If you think it is all about taking your dog for a walk down a few blocks, you are sadly mistaken. There are some dogs that need mental stimulation just as much as they need physical. Many pet owners would save much money in training their dogs if they would just give their dog the correct amount of exercise that he needs. Properly exercising a dog can eliminate his unruly behavior in the house. It can also cut down on his destructive behavior, excessive barking issues, and can also help you out with leash walking, too. Proper exercise can help out many other problem behaviors too, but those are the main ones. Please pay close attention to this topic because I will be talking about each breed group and what kind of exercise they need.

AKC- American Kennel Club

The AKC, which was established on September 17, 1884, put together seven groups into which some of the world's most popular dog breeds fit: Sporting, Non- sporting, Working, Herding, Terriers, Toys, and Hounds—these are the seven groups that the AKC uses to categorize the world's most recognized breeds. What group does your dog fall into? I would like to go through them with you one at a time and let you know certain characteristics and common habits that distinguish each breed. Knowing more about your dog's group will help you understand and train your dog better. Even if you have a mixed breed or a mutt, this part will still help you out.

> **Mixed breed** – a dog whose parents are from two different breeds, but the breeds are known.

> **Mutt** – a dog whose parents are from two or more different breeds and the breeds are **not** known.

The Sporting Group

Golden Retriever   Labrador retriever

Weimaraner   Pointer

Cocker Spaniel   Irish Setter

> ➤ These dogs are bred to chase and catch game—like birds—on and off land.

> ➤ Some of them are bred to be big and strong with much energy. They have good temperaments.

> ➤ The larger dogs in this group--Retrievers, Weimaraner, Setters, and the Pointers--are very insensitive dogs. Because of their high tolerance for pain, the large dogs in this group are good-natured around children, but at the same very difficult to correct. A child can pull the dog's ear, tail, or tongue and it will not phase the dog. Most owners that have these breeds usually have to upgrade to another collar. They usually use gentle leaders, choke collars, and sometimes prong collars. Unless you are sure about what you are doing, seek some

help from a professional trainer before using a choke or prong collar. You can injure your dog if you do not know what you are doing.

➢ The Spaniel part of this group is a little different in a way. Most of these dogs are sensitive. So this means that it is not difficult to correct them, but at the same they are not all that good with children. I am not saying that these are mean, aggressive dogs. If your child tries to pull the dog's tail, ears, or tongue, the dog will probably react. They are sensitive to that kind of stuff.

➢ The breeds in this group need their exercise. I cannot stress how important it is for them to release their energy. The dogs in this group are great to have when they have released their energy. A walk around the block is not enough for these dogs. I have the hardest problems with those clients who have dog breeds that are in this group. When I tell them what kind of exercise the dog is going to need, they look me as if my request is bizarre. Before getting a dog, you should know as much as possible about the breed that you are about to adopt. The proper exercise for the breeds in this group is run, run, run. If you do not have a fenced in yard, go to a dog park. You can also go to an empty tennis or basketball court early in the morning when no one is there. If you cannot let them run, walk the dog at *least* three to six miles—not in a week, but a day. If you do not exercise a dog in this group on any given day, you *will* notice a change in that same day – the destruction of your home. The windowsills, your coach, your plants, corners of your sheet rock, and much more will be destroyed. I have even seen one of these dogs chew a hole in a wall to get to the next room. If you do not channel your dog's energy by giving him outdoor exercise, it is just going to come out in the house. If you have a treadmill, use it to exercise your dog as well. The best exercise for your dog is to play with another dog, or for you to play fetch with him up a steep hill.

➢ Before you adopt a dog from this group, I hope you do your research and see if this type of dog matches your lifestyle.

The key to having one of these dogs is to know how to correct them and also to give them the maximum running time *each* day.

The Working Group

Rottweiler	Siberian Husky
Mastiff	Doberman Pincher

Portuguese Water dog	Boxer
Akita	St. Bernard
Newfoundland	Malamute

➢ The breeds in this group are bred to be dominant, and they sometimes end up dominating their owner. They are bred to take action. They are a little more independent than other breeds; for example, the Rottweiler is fearless. They do not need a human's help to protect their owner's property. One other example is the St. Bernard. They do not need anybody to help them rescue a human that is hidden under the snow of an avalanche.

➢ These dogs adjust to new surroundings well. They take some time out to study their new area and lie down and relax until something interesting occurs.

➢ I advise first time dog owners, or those who do not have much experience with dogs not to adopt a breed from this group. If you do not take this advice and decide to adopt one anyway, *please seek help from a reputable professional dog trainer.* Before adopting a breed from this group, do as much as you can to research the breed first. Like all purebreds, it is good to adopt these dogs from a breeder and not from a pet store. The breeder should be able to tell you the pedigree of the dog. A good breeder should have at least one of the parents present. It is likely that the puppies' temperament will be similar to the parents.

➤ Be firm when training these dogs. The breeds in this group will usually test your patience and consistency. You must be consistent. If anybody in the household feels afraid of the dog you plan to adopt, this might not be the breed for you.

➢ These dogs need to be socialized from an early age. The more you socialize a dog the less chance he will bite somebody—even you the owner.

➢ The St. Bernard and the Newfoundland only require about one or two miles walk each day. But the high energy dogs in this group such as Doberman Pinchers, the Boxers, and the Siberian Huskies need much more exercise than that. These dogs can do up to six miles and more in a day. Remember not to take a Boxer for long walks in the humid, hot weather.

➢ Most of the breeds in this group—such as the Rottweiler and the Siberian Husky—are versatile dogs in reference to weather. So if it is ever raining or if it is very cold outside, just make sure that you are okay, and take your dog outside no matter what kind of weather.

The Herding Group

German shepherd   Border collie

Australian Shepherd   Collie

Old English Sheep Dog   Bouvia

Komondor   Shiloh Shepherd

> ➤ These are very loyal dogs. They become your partners. They love being right by their owner's side. It is in these dogs to herd. You can have a Border Collie for three years and never trained him to herd. Then put some cattle in his path, and his herding instincts will come out. The herding group is very agile and smart. Keep this in mind if you ever plan on adopting one.

> ➤ The exercise for this group is different. Instead of just wearing them out physically, they also need mental

stimulation. A good way to keep them physically and mentally active is agility. Or you can take them for a three to six mile walk while your dog is walking in the perfect heel.

➤ This group will not behave well if bored. If you do not plan on keeping them active or giving them a job to do, then this type of dog is not for you.

The Toy Group

Chihuahua	Yorkshire Terrier
Maltese	Miniature Pincher
Pug	Japanese Chin
Miniature Poodle	Shihtzu
Brussels Griffon	Havenese

➢ The first thing that comes to my mind when I think about this group is their size. They are small dogs, and smaller dogs have smaller bladders. You might find it more difficult to potty train a toy breed. Many people that have these dogs get into the habit of just feeding their dog nothing but wet food. All that wet food is not good for their teeth. And wet food has water in it; so if you are trying to be successful with housebreaking your dog, you might want to stay away from all the wet food.

➢ The biggest thing that hinders most of these dogs from getting trained is usually their owners. This group usually gets much free affection from their owner. Remember the more free affection you show to a dog, the more they will walk all over you. Most pet owners let this group of dogs get away with so much because they always say the dog is their little baby and treat him as such. I have also seen these dogs in strollers when the dog has four healthy legs. There is no reason why these dogs should not have rules in their lives. These dogs are more adorable when they are trained. Just watch how much force you put into each correction.

➤ The good thing about these dogs is that you gain entrance into many more places than with other breeds. Wherever you take your dog, make sure he uses his four legs as much as possible.

➤ This group, just like all other groups, needs to be socialized as much as possible. I am sure you have heard of the phrase "ankle biters". They really will do that if they are under socialized. These dogs are also known as "lap dogs". They are mainly bred to be a companion. They like to spend a lot of time with their owners. If you are the type of owner that has to be away from home all day, this is not your breed.

➤ These dogs need exercise too. To wear my Yorkie out, I have to walk her six miles. There is nothing like a well-exercised dog.

The Hound Group

Scent	Sight
Beagle	Borzoi
Bloodhound	Afghan Hound
Fox Hound	Grey Hound
Black and Tan Coon Hound	Saluki

> ➤ Most people looking into this group, or that already have a dog in the group do not know that there are two different types of hounds—sight and scent hounds. Training can be difficult based upon the type of hound that is being trained. The scent hounds will pull when on the leash, and both the scent and sight hounds can run far away if they get loose. This group is bred to hunt. Part of the group is bred to hunt by sight and the other by scent. Some of the scent hounds can pick up a scent that is four

days old. The sight hounds are bred to be fast so that they can catch up togame like rabbits. The Greyhound is the fastest running dog in the world. To adopt some hounds, you are required to have a fenced in yard.

➢ Like I said earlier the scent hounds were bred to use their nose. If you are not going to use them for tracking, then you should do exercises that allow them to use their nose. Hide and seek is a great game for them or you can have them search for objects.

➢ A tool that can really help you out with walking most of the dogs in this group is the Gentle Leader.

➢ Do your research before adopting a dog in this group. I would say the most popular hound in this group that people adopt as a companion is the Beagle.

The Terrier Group

Jack Russell Terrier

West Highland White Terrier

Soft coated Wheaten Terrier

Fox Terrier

Rat Terrier

Staffordshire Terrier

Airedale Terrier

Bull Terrier

➤ The first thing that comes to mind with this group is that they are really good at balancing themselves on their back legs and that they are very fast. This group usually has jumping issues. The dogs in this group were bred to catch game, as well. They were bred to chase rodents above and underground. So if you adopt a terrier and he has a digging problem, do not be surprised.

➤ It is important to exercise these dogs. Sometimes you will feel that nothing is going to work to wear the dog out. Their energy level is extremely high. To release their energy, walk them at least six miles. Playing a good game of fetch outside can do the trick, too. Believe it or not, there is also a way to exercise a terrier in the house. You can blow up a balloon, and he will try to catch it. He will make the balloon bounce high and as he tries to jump for it as it comes back down to him, he will bounce it up again. Supervise this kind of playtime.

The Non-Sporting Group

Dalmatian

French Bull dog

Bichon Frise

Poodle

English Bull dog

Keeshond

➢ The breeds in this group do not really have anything in common with each other. But each dog has something in common with breeds in other groups; for example, the Dalmatian can do things like the dogs in the sporting group. They also need much exercise. And for the Bichon, I would give you the same tips that I gave you for the Toy group.

➢ The main thing I would advise is that you research the breed before you adopt. Most of the dogs in this group are different from each other and bred for different reasons.

I hope this information helps you with the breed of dog that you either have or are about to adopt. It was fun having you and your beautiful dog in my class. Keep your head up and don't give up on your dog. You can train any dog, if you have the proper technique and time needed. For any questions, you can contact me by email at cbrown562@hotmail.com.

Before you go, I would like to help you out with remembering some of the things that you read by giving you one last quiz.

Quiz # 6

1. When should you switch a dog's food from puppy to adult?

2. Can the wrong food affect a dog with training?

3. Is the settle command a control behavior position?

4. True/False: You should wrestle your dog down to the floor when putting him/her into the settle position.

5. True/False: It does not matter if you exercise your dog or not.

6. How many breed groups are in the AKC?

7. What does AKC mean?

8. What foods are toxic to dogs?

9. Is there a difference between mutt and mix breed dogs?

10. How do you work on the Settle command for homework?

Answers:

1. You should switch to adult when the dog is a year old unless the vet tells you otherwise.
2. Yes
3. Yes
4. False
5. False
6. Seven
7. American Kennel Club
8. Chocolate, Onions, Grapes, and Raisins
9. Yes
10. You have to try to make your dog hit the position while he is doing the house race track.